INTRODUCTION

Brian D. Dillon

All archaeological writing can be placed in two basic categorical divisions: that which reports on or interprets actual archaeological discoveries, and that which proposes the ways and means by which new discoveries can be made or interpreted. Archaeological writing on systems theory, simulation, and method (sometimes mislabeled methodology) obviously belongs to the second category. Usually lacking in such writing is a sense of practicality, which should be taken to mean the implementation of a theory or method in an actual field or laboratory situation. This lack may be understandable, for it is only in a practical situation that a new idea can be evaluated in terms of actual archaeological success. Should archaeological writing about the ways and means of research be a topical triumvirate featuring theory, method, and practice? In my opinion it should, and the following papers bear witness to the value of practical considerations within the field. They are useful and instructive because they address real problems from the world of real archaeology, and propose real solutions for them that have been proven successful through trial and error.

Practical archaeology, therefore, is a means to an end, that end being the advance of objective archaeological knowledge. As such, it stands little danger of becoming an end in of itself (as have method and theory), because practical archaeology is the study of what works in a specific context. It is in danger, however, of being accorded only parochial importance until it can be shown that what can be practiced successfully in one archaeological context can also be applied to another one. Specific archaeological goals will differ depending upon geographical location, chronological time frame, cultural background, and intellectual focus of the archaeologist and his audience, but the mastery of practical archaeology becomes the common denominator upon which archaeological success of any kind is predicated. Practical expertise will enable the archaeologist to leap the hurdles that stand between the desire to do archaeology and the hope of making important discoveries, and the ability to fulfill that desire.

This volume does report to some extent on archaeological results but it is much more closely focused upon archaeological problem-solving in a variety of research contexts, both in the field and the laboratory. The practical ideas presented herein are directed towards the field archaeologist in order to expand his available range of research tools with which to intensify, broaden, or prolong his data recovery capabilities and to make his investigation of the past more efficient. Efficiency is again not an end in itself, only the means towards finishing archaeological tasks with greater dispatch, less expenditure of funds or energy, and recovery of greater amounts of information. Archaeological efficiency in practical terms should produce a surplus, therefore, of time, money, and labor over archaeological inefficiency; with this surplus the archaeologist can collect additional evidence or spend additional time on interpretation, and the size of the data sample and firmness of the conclusions reached can be improved.

Each of the following papers is an exercise in practical archaeology because it results from its writer's personal familiarity with an archaeological problem situation (or situations) from the real world, and the solution or solutions proposed have had success in actual application. Studies of settlement patterns, for example, are current fare for undergraduate instruction in archaeology (and often within geography departments as well); most good students can rattle off a long list of archaeological site layout characteristics and define and contrast "camps," "villages," and "cities" in artifactually or architecturally quantitative terms, citing nearest-neighbor theory and chi-square diagrams as evidence. The same student will probably be singularly unsucessful if asked to actually make a planimetric map of an amphorous aggregate of crumbling adobe brick walls in the desert or to calculate the height and surface dimensions of a pyramid in the rain forest, for a facility with theoretical models is no substitute for practical training. The two papers on mapping, by Van Horn and Murray and by Whitley, help to codify such practical considerations and provide many useful shortcuts to success in field mapping of archaeological sites and in precisely localizing artifacts in their discovered associations. Such skills are the most basic prerequisites for any kind of spatial analysis of archaeological remains.

If the precise localization of associated artifacts and features is important in mapping, where an essentially two-dimensional characterization of reality is produced, it is even more important in excavation, where three-dimensional reconstuctions become necessary. Stratigraphic interpretation and the understanding of superpositional sequences necessitates absolute vertical control no less than horizontal accuracy, and the paper by Winans and Winans provides us with an easily constructed apparatus and working method by which such goals can be achieved. A lack of facility with taking measurements in field excavations can have disastrous results for both archaeology and paleontology. An apparently disarticulated mammoth in the American Great Basin, for example, has very important implications for the question of how the continent was originally populated, and we would like to be certain that the transposition of the bones is the result of manipulation by early man rather than the result of a field recorder who could not keep his line level and his tape straight.

Since the 1940's chemical and physical testing of archaeological deposits and of artifacts has come to be standard investigative procedure, but most archaeologists tend to think of such uses of applied science as almost exclusively laboratory-based. Van Horn and Murray's second paper shows how by systematic common sense the chemical laboratory can be brought to the archaeological site itself; through the application of a simple and easily reproducible process artifactual material can be "unlocked" from a context that was previously loath to yield it up.

2

CONTENTS

Illustration Credits

J.P. Brock: (page) 12; B.D. Dillon: 63, 65, 70, 101, 103, 104, 106, 109, 112, 119; C. Donnan: 34, 35; M.C. Johnson: 92; W.D. Mc Cawley: 9, 29; W.A. Sawyer: 30; L.J. Tartaglia: 36, 37, 38, 41, 42; A.V. Van Horn: 11; D.M. Van Horn: 8, 27, 28; D.M. Whitley: 17; M.C. Winans: 47, 48, 49, 50, 51, 54; R.C. Winans: 53, 56, 57. Design and layout by Brian D. Dillon. Cover illustration by Ross C. Winans.

ISBN: 0-917956-42-7

In the laboratory itself, archaeology has made giant strides in just the past two decades. Technology borrowed from other fields in the form of electron microscopy and neutron activation have been applied to long-standing archaeological problems with singularly successful results. Some questions previously considered unanswerable, such as the ultimate points of origin of imported items in foreign contexts, can now be resolved using such advanced technology. Unfortunately, such specialized machinery is relatively uncommon and its use is still beyond the financial means of many archaeologists and certainly most students. The X-ray machine, on the other hand, has been with us since 1895, is commonly available in most large cities in most countries, and can even sometimes be purchased used. Tartaglia's demonstration of some of the archaeological potentials of X-ray analysis underline the fact that technology need not be expensive or experimental in order to assist in practical archaeological research. This consideration becomes increasingly important to the scholar who cannot bring his specimens home for analysis in his own lab, but must study them in their country of origin.

The final three papers, by Meighan and Dillon, Banks and Dillon, and Dillon, all deal with problems and solutions of a logistical nature that are commonly encountered by field archaeologists. Archaeological logistics have received almost no publication exposure, despite the fact that basic problems of supply, communication, and transportation beset every field project and perhaps combine to form the most universal archaeological common denominator. Few archaeologists and fewer neophytes still can be expected in the 1980's to make commonsense logistical decisions, for very few have a background that includes any practical experience outside of the academic milieu. While most archaeologists dream of getting to an untouched archaeological location and making startling discoveries, few are willing to begin such a project unless air passage is available to the point of discovery or a freeway has gone through. The practical archaeologist, however, knows that solving logistical problems rapidly and efficiently means that four or five research projects can be completed annually instead of just one, and that more resources can be devoted to doing archaeology than to preparing for doing it. Logistical self-sufficiency makes the archaeologist more mobile, saves him more time, energy, and money, and lets him go further in his analysis of recovered materials. The cumulative result of such self-reliance is that more archaeology gets done, and done more completely.

Although many more projects are being proposed today than just five years ago, the sources of funds for which these are in competition have dwindled to a fraction of what was available a decade ago. Now as never before the research archaeologist must economize and must solve practical problems himself instead of hiring a specialist or forgoing portions of his research. If his working schedule does not permit his direct involvement in some of the more "grass-roots" activities necessary to the progress of his research venture, then he should at least have the experience adequate for training a willing graduate student, workman, or volunteer to handle specific extractive, recording, analytical, or logistical tasks.

Much attention is given to the "strategy" of archaeology today, by which is meant the grand scale objectives and potentialities of certain kinds of research; concomitantly, little is heard about archaeological tactics. Practical archaeology then, provides a partial solution for this situation. It takes the researcher many steps beyond theory, for while the one only proposes, the other disposes. By underlining the usefulness of practical archaeology, one should not conclude that all other kinds of archaeology are necessarily "impractical", only that through application, practical archaeology can bring us closer to concrete discoveries than any other form of research.

TRANSIT CONTROLLED SURFACE COLLECTING

David M. Van Horn and John R. Murray

Introduction

The emergence of the field of "consulting" archaeology has led to the development of faster and more efficient methods of data recovery. The professional consultant must provide his client with more than an academically acceptable field program. He must also consider how the work can be accomplished with the greatest speed and the least cost. In the following paragraphs, we examine the efficiency of several surface collection methods in terms of speed and accuracy.

Traditionally, large-scale surface collection projects have been tedious and time consuming tasks due principally to the problem of accurately recording the proveniences of the finds. The most common method entails laying a grid over the site in whatever size squares seems most appropriate and then collecting the cultural material situated within the squares (often only a sample of the squares are collected). Proveniences of the collected items are recorded in terms of the coordinates of the squares. There are several needless difficulties which are encountered when using such a method.

The first involves layout out of the grid itself. Let us assume that an archaeologist wishes to collect 100 percent of the cultural material from a site that can be enclosed within a 100 x 100 meter grid. We shall also assume that the grid square size will be 5 x 5 meters. Forty-two stakes and 300 meters of string will be required to lay out one row of the grid. If the ground is hard, the stakes may be difficult to drive. Vegetation and topography may interfere with the alignment of the strings. It could easily require one-half day for two people to lay only one-tenth of the grid area. Assuming that the work could be accomplished at twice the rate after the first row is laid out, four additional man-days would be required to complete the grid and nothing would have been collected (using the method described below, over 800 items could have been collected and recorded over the same period of time).

The grid system is fraught with other problems. Especially important is the fact that the proveniences recorded are only as accurate as the grid square size. In the example set forth above, the location of an item is known only in terms of a 25 square meter area. Using smaller squares improves the accuracy but greatly compounds the logistical problems entailed in laying the grid out. In the case of a small concentration of objects, the position of one item relative to the next is entirely lost. When the grid results are mapped, only an abstract picture of the site appears since it can only be illustrated in terms of the density of objects found within the squares.

A better system from an accuracy point-of-view entails collecting the artifacts after having measured their distance and angle relative to one or more datum stakes. Measuring is performed with a tape and compass or protractor. This technique was used by Dillon when he was unable to lay out a grid because of off-road vehicle activity (Dillon, n.d.: 4f) However, Dillon describes it as "laborious" and it is clear that such a method is no faster than the grid system unless one is dealing with only a few items which require collecting. Moreover, such a method would be completely unfeasible on a large site where thousands of items had to be collected.

A transit is designed to facilitate measuring distances and angles. Optical location of each item can be performed in a fraction of the time required to measure by hand and may feasibly be used on any site of any size. The potential for accuracy sometimes excels that of measuring by hand.

Transit Controlled Surface Collecting

Using a transit in determining the proveniences of surface finds is not a new or a unique idea. However, transit controlled collections are usually restricted to operations in which only a few items are to be collected (e.g. less than 200) because the instrument operators do not know how to use their transit efficiently and because the collection team does not function at maximum speed. We have been performing transit controlled surface collections since 1977 and this experience has led us to a refined system which is both efficient and accurate. The system of collection and mapping will be described first and a discussion of some of the results will follow.

Artifact Location and Flagging

Cultural items to be collected are first located by a team of three persons (who will also perform the collection operation). The team walks in parallel transects until the entire site has been covered. Each person carries a bundle of 1/16th inch diameter welding rods with surveyor's flagging tied to loops bent in the ends of the rods. He inserts one of these "flags" into the ground next to each item to be collected. If the ground is very hard, the staff should be equipped with ice picks for pre-punching the hole in which the flag will be placed. If the site is very large and thousands of objects are to be collected, it may be flagged and collected one portion at a time, leaving a line of flags in place to delineate the area which remains to be collected.

Collection Procedure

Once a site or part of a site has been flagged, collection may begin. This is per—

Archaeological **Associates LTD**

Page _____

Datum _____

Date _____

Number	Description	Distance	Azimuth	Elevation	Conversion

Figure 1: Heading for the transit note form. The "conversion" column is used by the cartographer for recording the map-scale distance.

formed by the same three people who performed the flagging operation. They will become (1) the transit operator, (2) the stadia rod man, and (3) the "bag" man. The transit operator stands at the instrument which is set up over the most appropriate datum location. The rod man places the stadia directly behind the object to be collected and the transit operator locates the rod, recording the coordinates on a form designed for the purpose. At the same time, the rod man removes the flag and the bag man places the object in a zip-lock plastic bag. The bag may be numbered on the spot or pre-numbered bags may be used. The bag man then places the object in a duffle bag fitted with a shoulder strap and calls out the number and identity of the object (chipped stone, ground stone, shell, etc.) to the transit man who records this information on his form (fig. 1). Thus, the transit notes include the number, identity and coordinates of each item collected. By the time the bag man has finished, the rod man has moved to the nearest object remaining to be collected and the cycle is repeated. Walkie talkies can be very helpful on large sites or on very windy days. We use Realistic model TRC-201's fitted with short flexible antennas and home-made leather holsters so that the transit operator can hear the bag man's number and identification of the object without encumbering either of his hands. These walkie talkies are relatively inexpensive (about $70 each), can be recharged, and offer adequate range and power life for a full day's collecting

Once the team has become accustomed to working together, it is possible to obtain and record the coordinates of an object in 5-6 seconds (faster than the rod and bag man can collect the objects). This speed is achieved by using a short-cut in calculating the distance of the object.

When performing a normal transit shot, the operator first levels the telescope and then focuses on the stadia rod. He calculates the distance by subtracting the bottom cross-hair reading on the stadia from the top cross-hair reading (fig. 2a) thus obtaining the difference between the two which, when multiplied by 100, yields the distance of the rod from the transit. The telescope is set on level before making the calculations because the operator desires the true linear distance from the rod to the transit--any variation in the telescope angle from absolute level introduces an error in the resulting distance as shown in Figure 3 (i.e., it makes the object appear to be slightly farther away than it actually is). However, this also results in the cross-hairs in the telescope being placed at arbitrary levels relative to the increments on the rod. Thus the operator must deal with clumsy figures and then subtract one from the other in order to derive his distance as shown in Figure 2a.

With our technique we ignore leveling the telescope and the operator immediately sets the lower cross-hair on an even increment on the stadia (e.g., 1.0 m as fig. 2b). For distances of less than 100 meters, the number of centimeters between top and bottom cross-hairs may then be read directly from the stadia with no subtraction or uneven figures. For example, if the bottom cross-hair is placed on the one-meter increment and the top cross-hair reads 1.14 meters (fig. 2b), it is immediately apparent that the object is 14 meters distant.

As mentioned above, elevating or de-elevating the telescope introduces an error into the distance reading. Thus, it is essential to know what error is being introduced in order to be certain that it is in an insignificant range. The error (E) is equal to the cosine of the angle on the telescope (a) times the distance being shot (d):

$$E = Cos \ a \ x \ d$$

The following table provides the cosines of a few angles and the resulting errors at a distance of 100 meters:

Angle	Cosine	Error (cms)	% Error
1°	0.9998	2.0	0.02
2°	0.9994	4.0	0.06
3°	0.9986	14.0	0.14
4°	0.9976	24.0	0.24
5°	0.9962	38.0	0.38
6°	0.9945	55.0	0.55
7°	0.9925	75.0	0.75
8°	0.9900	100.0	1.00

Thus, an angle of 3° on the telescope introduces an error of 14 cm at 100 meters (0.14%). For surface collection and mapping purposes, such an error will almost always be entirely insignificant. An angle of 8° will have to be introduced before a 1% error results. As long as the operator is aware of the error he is introducing, he can determine whether it is tolerable and if so, shoot objects in a small fraction of the time required to level the telescope and then calculate the distance from arbitrary points on the stadia scale. We have found that it is rare that the telescope will be elevated or de-elevated more than 4 or 5 degrees. In the event that absolute accuracy is required, it is much faster simply to record the angle shown on the telescope protractor rather than level the telescope and figure the distance in the field. The simple trigonometric formula presented above can be used to calculate the actual linear distance back in the laboratory.

There is virtually no comparison between the grid method and the transit controlled method in terms of both speed and accurary. In fact, smaller surface scatters can be completely surface collected in about the same time required to simply lay out a grid. The transit method offers the advantage of recording the exact location of each object with any degree of accuracy required in a matter of seconds. A preliminary catalogue of the finds is a by-product of the procedure and each item is bagged with its catalogue number when the collection is complete. All of the equipment can be re-used and the data enable the cartographer to plot out an actual map of the locations of the finds at any scale on any type of map.

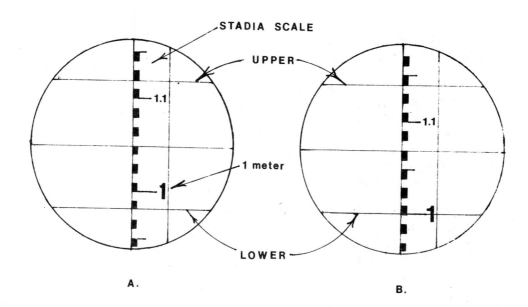

Figure 2: *Views of stadia as seen through the telescope. A: With the telescope level, the upper and lower cross-hairs fall at arbitrary increments on the stadia scale. B: With the lower cross-hair placed on an even increment, the distance reading is greatly facilitated.*

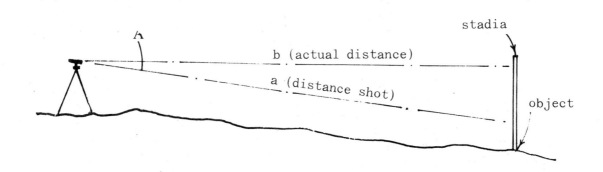

Figure 3: *Diagram showing the error introduced by moving the transit telescope away from absolute level.*

Cartography

One of the greatest advantages of the transit controlled surface collecting system is that it provides data for drawing a scale map of the scatter as it actually appears. This is accomplished by simply locating the transit datum(s) on the base map and then plotting the angles and distances from the transit notes. The distances must be changed to the scale of the map but this is easily accomplished with any adding machine or pocket calculator. Calculators equipped with constant keys are particularly

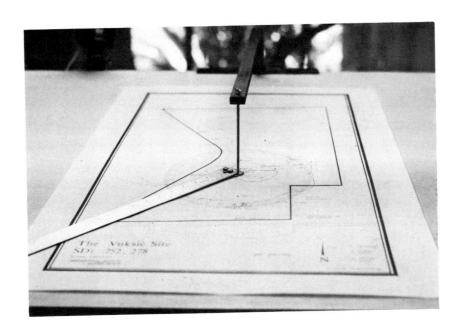

Figure 4: Home-made plotting equipment. The ruler pivots around the adjustable pin held by the iron bar at top; the bar is fastened to the drawing table with C-clamps. The 360° mylar protractor shows as a circular shadow under the mylar sheet which bears the surface scatter plot.

useful for converting the distances to map scale since one need only figure the factor which will bring the distances down to map scale and enter this factor into the device as the constant. This avoids the necessity of re-entering the factor each time a new distance is converted and thereby saves considerable time. In fact, it is possible to convert several thousand distances per hour when a device with a constant key is used. Forms such as that shown in Figure 1 are convenient in that they already have a column for the converted (map scale) distance. Symbols may be used on the map for different types of items collected (e.g. an "X" for chipped stone, a small circle for shell, etc.). Alternatively, the numbers assigned to the objects can also be used although a very large-scale map might be necessary since the numbers may tend to overlap.

Nothing more complicated than a protractor and a ruler is actually required to do the plotting. On the other hand, a computer equipped with a plotter can be used if such a device is available. We have not generally had the benefit of access to a computer and have worked out several simple ways of performing the plotting by hand in an expeditious manner. The simplest is simply to use a marine navigational protractor which already has a pivoting ruler attached to the center of a 360° protractor. The rulers on these devices may be in increments designed to accommodate the standard scale of nautical charts but this problem can be overcome by simply gluing or taping a ruler of the desired scale over the ruler attached to the protractor.

If it is anticipated that many maps will be drawn up, it may be worthwhile to build a special plotting device such as that shown in Figure 4. This instrument is an iron bar which extends out over the drawing table and holds an adjustable pivot point which is located directly over the center of a 360° protractor. The latter is

a mylar copy which can be made from a plastic protractor at any blueprint repro-
duction facility for about $5. The mylar protractor is simply fastened onto the
drawing surface with tape. The mylar or acetate sheet which will bear the plot is
then placed over the protractor in such a way that the transit datum on the sheet is
centered on the protractor. The pivot point and the ruler are then placed over the
same point. The cartographer may then simply pivot the ruler to the correct angle,
find the distance on the ruler scale and plot the location of the object. Several
hundred points may be plotted in an hour using this simple homemade set-up.

Discussion

The procedure described above will produce a map of publishable quality without
requiring special computer skills or expensive equipment. Careful draftsmanship
will result in a map of sufficient accuracy for establishing legal boundaries such as
the open-space easements which are frequently used in avoidance type mitigation
procedures often connected with environmental work. Moreover, the resulting maps
are often useful for site interpretation since they provide an excellent idea of the
actual dispersion patterns of objects. Areas of concentration of a particular category of object may be readily discerned. In some cases, the density of surface material is a reflection of the presence or absence of a subsurface deposit. The surface collection map can be of great assistance in formulating excavation strategy in
such instances.

Occasionally, a large site with many surface items may require so much time to
surface collect that it is feasible to collect only a sample of the material using the
grid system. This kind of sampling procedure may often be entirely avoided in
favor of a 100% surface collection when the transit controlled technique is introduced.
Our organization has encountered a number of such instances. Perhaps the most
notable involved a late Intermediate milling station situated in the foothills of the
Santa Ana Mountains, Orange County. The site is situated on a partially eroding
terrace about 100 feet above Aliso Creek. Erosion combined with many years of
agricultural plowing had resulted in the exposure of approximately 3500 cultural
items spread over an area covering about two acres. Finds consisted principally of
chipped stone, ground stone, hammerstones, and fire-cracked rock. These were
located and the artifacts collected using the transit controlled system described
above. They were then plotted using the iron bar and mylar protractor shown in
Figure 4. Finds were very dense and consequently the categories of items were
plotted on separate mylar overlays (Fig. 5). The results were useful in two respects.

First, the scatters of all items permitted us to accurately determine which portions of the site were heavily eroding and which probably included an entirely
buried deposit. That is, those areas which yielded heavy concentrations of surface
finds were deflated while those which did not were likely to retain depositional in-
tegrity. Subsequent excavation of a portion of the site confirmed this conclusion
and therefore, excavations were concentrated in a small area where surface finds
were sparse. An intact activity surface was eventually uncovered here (Van Horn
and Murray n.d.).

A reduction of the fire-cracked rock scatter is shown in Figure 5. The plots
for the chipped stone and ground stone items were similar in shape and density with
a single exception. This is the rather dense concentration of thermally altered rock
shown in the lower left hand corner of the rock scatter. Clearly, this concentration
is not random. It was interpreted as representing the former location of a roasting
pit. Excavation of a unit within the concentration showed that the topsoil was less
than 20 centimeters deep in this location, and plow scars were clearly evident in

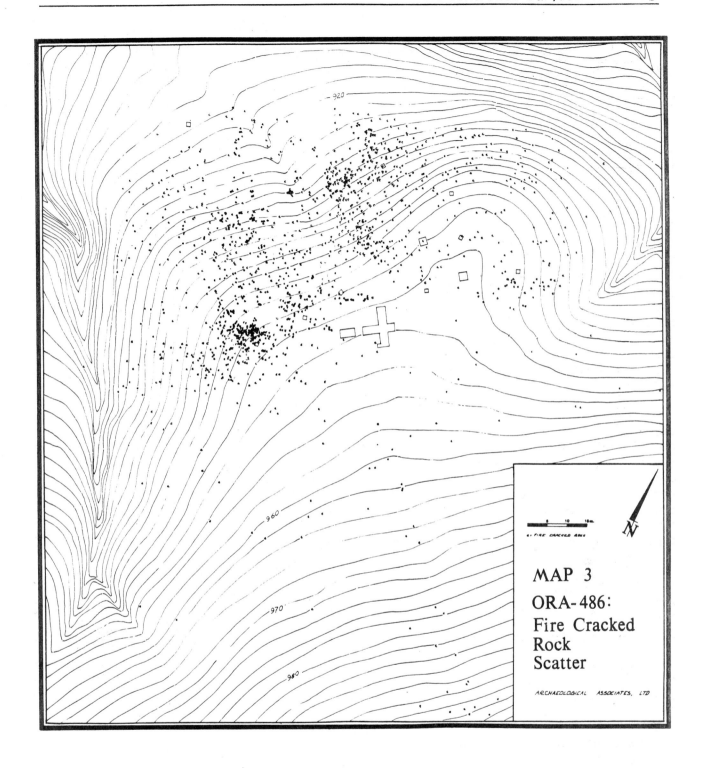

MAP 3
ORA-486:
Fire Cracked
Rock
Scatter

ARCHAEOLOGICAL ASSOCIATES, LTD

Figure 5: Map of the fire-cracked rock scatter at CA-Ora-486; note the concentration at left center. Rectilinear areas are excavation units. (From Van Horn and Murray, n.d.).

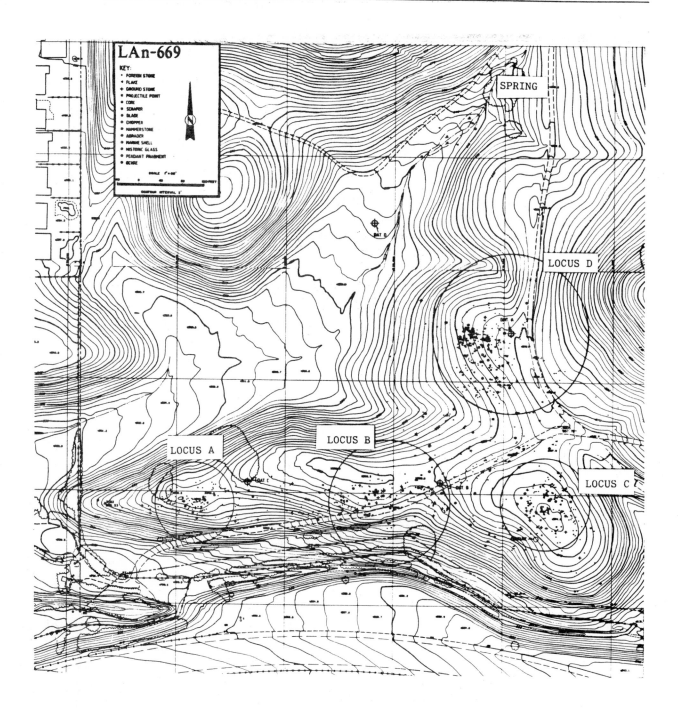

Figure 6: Surface scatter at the Daon site (LAn-669). The habitation deposit is buried under recent sediments around the spring at top. The original plot scale is 1"=40'.

the hardpan below. The roasting pit would have almost certainly remained unknown to us had we not plotted out the location of each surface item. Also, it is evident that there was once at least one additional roasting pit since the scatter of fire-cracked rock on the right half of the plot must have originally comprised such a feature.

A second interesting instance of the usefulness of transit controlled surface collection was encountered at the Daon site (LAn-669) located in Las Virgenes Canyon, Los Angeles County. This is a late Chumash camp consisting of an entirely buried habitation area around a small spring accompanied by surface scatters on a ridge and terrace to the south (Van Horn and Brock n.d.). A reduction of the surface collection plot is shown in Figure 6. It is evident from the plot that we were dealing with a series of four separate loci and we drew circles of arbitrary radius around each. We then calculated the range of transit coordinates encompassed by each circle and ascribed either a locus status of non-locus status to each of the surface items collected. We found that there were differences in the character of the items found at each locus. Locus A yielded relatively few items which included a mortar fragment and a pestle, Locus B included a preponderance of flaked items interpreted as pulping planes, Locus C yielded a preponderance of manos and flakes, while Locus D yielded an array of items including a pendant fragment, steatite bead fragment, large sandstone grooved abrading stone for tool manufacture, stone bowl fragment and several pestle fragments. Excavation of a test unit at Locus D yielded a number of small fused shale and chert pressure flakes suggesting biface manufacture at this locus.

We think that the finds at Locus D are more reflective of male-oriented activities while those on the ridge to the south (A-C) indicate food processing or a female orientation. Whatever the activities which were taking place at the four loci, it became clear that each represented an activity area and that actual habitation only took place around the spring where excavation has yielded ecofactual material in considerable quantities. We doubt that an adequate picture of these activity areas could be developed without actual plotting of the find locations. It may be worth noting that the entire surface collection shown in Figure 6 was performed by three individuals in one day and that the cartography required only one man-day.

Conclusions

Transit controlled surface collecting is a fast and inexpensive method for obtaining an excellent rendition of a scatter of cultural material. In most instances, it produces more accurate results in less time and for less cost than the grid system. Use of a compass and measuring tape can be used as a substitute in small areas where there are no obstructions but otherwise use of a transit is best. However, the transit operator must use short-cuts in order for the collection to be performed with optimal efficiency. A well-controlled collection could virtually be replaced on the site without significant change from the original scatter configuration.

PRACTICAL MAPPING FOR THE FIELD ARCHAEOLOGIST

David M. Whitley

Introduction

Mapping archaeological sites ranks with taking field notes, completing excavation level records, and drawing stratigraphic profiles as an essential, albeit often tedious, part of data collection. The importance of this task is emphasized by a few recent publications devoted exclusively to the cartography of major archaeological sites: the Teotihuacan Map (Millon, Drewitt, and Cowgill 1973) and the Chan Chan Map (Moseley and Mackey 1974). Most archaeological mapping efforts are, luckily, not as monumental as these examples, yet it can be said that the fieldwork on any site is never complete until the map has been made. The purpose of this short article is to provide a few practical pointers to the archaeologist faced with the job of making the map. It is based on my own experience as a clerk in a building supply store selling surveying equipment, and as a freelance cartographer who has done archaeological mapping in California, the Great Basin, and Mesoamerica.

Archaeologists too often have been poorly equipped, in the literal and in the figurative sense, to make a quick and an accurate field map. Clearly, projects such as those of Millon and Moseley require techniques more sophisticated than those discussed here. However, the vast majority of research and contract archaeology studies require relatively simple maps that can be made by the average ambulatory graduate student or the advanced undergraduate in a few days' time or less, and it is to this audience that the suggestions that follow are addressed. The chief considerations are of accuracy in mapping, means of getting the most out of your budget when buying mapping equipment, and, finally, shortcuts to planimetric data reduction.

Accuracy in Mapping

It is important to recognize that a map is a generalization of reality. Except in rare cases, it is an approximation of geographical and cultural features, and is not intended to be an exact rendering of their distributions. A map, therefore, differs from a blueprint, which is a much more exact representation of an object. Consequently, there is a point at which an obsession with accuracy can become counterproductive, due to the limitations inherent in the mapping equipment available to the average archaeologist, the human error that is always present in data collecting, and the error that is introduced when mapping data are reduced so as to sufficiently reproduce them as a page-size illustration. It is important to keep these last three factors in mind because they will determine the degree of accuracy that should be attempted in your mapping effort.

In this regard I am reminded of a situation that is perhaps familiar to many. A particular archaeologist made a series of maps of several sites that I was working at; we were digging 1 by 1 meter square pits and the archaeologists making the map dutifully mapped in each corner of each 1-meter square unit. Once the map was completed, the sides of each pit were inked in, yet the pits were drawn exactly according to the mapping data. This resulted in a weird variety of trapezoidal shapes that were anything but the squares of the original excavation pits. Why? The mapper would probably respond by stating that the pits were not square which, in this case, I know to be false. Rather, the equipment being used had an accuracy that was only within 1 foot per 100 feet (or, potentially as much as a 30 percent divergence on each corner of a 1-meter square pit) and, at the distances involved, accurate measurements of points one meter apart would have required azimuthal readings taken to the second, while the transit employed was graduated only to five second readings.

The point here is that a good field mapper recognizes the limitations of his equipment, his own limitations in accuracy, and the ultimate use to which his mapping data is to be put. On a site of any size (e.g. over 30 meters in any direction) that is to be illustrated on an 8½ x 11" page, no real detail can be provided for any feature that is only a meter square in size. A 1 by 1 meter pit, for example, need only be mapped at one point (e.g. in its exact middle or at a specific corner) and rightly should be illustrated as a point symbol (for example, a small dot, star, or triangle) on the final map. To do otherwise is to imply an accuracy that probably has not been achieved.

The recognition that a map is a generalization is, of course, no excuse for sloppy or inaccurate work. However, bear in mind that the degree of accuracy on a U.S.G.S. 7.5 minute topographical quadrangle is 20 feet (that is, any contour or feature on the map is within 20 feet of its actual location on the ground). If the U.S.G.S. can accept this degree of accuracy on their maps while using the latest photogrammetric techniques, the archaeologist should then accept that generalization is unavoidable in a map. Hence, in the strictly cartographic sense, the scale of a map is never stated as "1 = 100,000," or "one inch equals 100,000," Rather, it is "1: 100,000," or "one inch is equivalent to 100,000 inches"—an approximate relationship.

In general, as mapping data is reduced to a size appropriate for illustration, each item to be placed on the map will occupy a proportionately larger amount of space, and the amount of information that can be shown per unit area decreases in geometrical progression. Cartographers have worked out mathematical statements expressing the relationship between map scale and amount of detail that can be reasonably portrayed (cf. Topfer and Pillewizer 1966; Robinson and Sale 1969). These need not concern us here. However, based on the reduction in detail that can be expressed on maps as indicated by these equations, it is obvious that a similar situation exists as regards accuracy of portrayal. Accuracy in a drafted map is, in a very real sense, a function of the amount of detail that can be drawn in. Hence, the average site map, when illustrated on a single page, is hardly an accurate rendering of the locational relationships of the objects and features that it portrays.

Recognition of your mapping needs and the required degree of accuracy is the first step in preparing for any mapping project, and these determine the amount of effort which should be invested in the task. To map in every single artifact found in an excavation with a transit and a stadia rod, for example, is getting to be a common practice in certain archaeological regions. Unfortunately, given the accuracy of most transit/stadia combinations, archaeologists would achieve much greater accuracy in determining exact provenience with the use of a line level and a surveyor's tape. Equally important, this greater accuracy might be obtained in much shorter time, with much less effort, and at substantially less equipment expense. The use of a transit and a stadia rod, as noted above, results in a margin of error in distance determinations that is basically unacceptable if the interest is in exact provenience. The kind of equipment to be used in mapping is a major concern, but one should not, however, be mislead by high prices and sophisticated looking equipment. Cost and complexity are not a necessary indication of accuracy, nor of applicability to average archaeological needs.

The Practical Side of Mapping Equipment

Most archaeologists working out of academic institutions inherit field equipment from previous archaeological projects. Consequently, they have to make do with someone else's choice in mapping tools, which may or may not have been good. My perspective is that in most situations such as this two or three times as much money as necessary was expended on the equipment purchased. The resulting mapping kit ends up metaphorically being a Cadillac with high-speed overdrive, when all the archaeologist needs is a pickup truck that he never takes out of first gear.

Relatively accurate maps of most sites can be made with less than $200.00 worth of equipment in 1982 dollars, and this budget can be fit into almost any grant or contract proposal and afforded by most individuals. The basic mapping kit is the Brunton compass, a surveyor's tape, and a book of stadia reduction tables. With these three items a reasonably accurate contour map can be made that is adequate for most archaeological purposes. Obviously, more equipment will be needed if you want to map a site like Teotihuacan; but in such a case it would be wise to enlist the services of a civil engineer. Some additional instruments may be desired if you are doing a substantial amount of mapping or are attemping to obtain exact provenience.

The Brunton compass is truly a "pocket transit," and is without question the most useful piece of mapping equipment an archaeologist can purchase. My own Brunton is one that my father bought as a geology student in 1935, and 47 years later I am still using it. The advantages of the Brunton over other compasses is that it has sights for accurate aiming, a level to indicate horizontal reading, and a vernier for taking vertical angle readings (a feature which makes it useful for

16

Figure 1: (Above): A basic mapping kit, including Brunton compass, Lietz 50 meter utility tape, and book of stadia reduction tables. (Below) A level-transit and stadia rod in use, Ventura County, California, 1982.

making contour maps). Additionally, a light-weight tripod can be obtained for a Brunton. As of 1982, the cost of one of these compasses hovers around $130.00.

The next item essential to any mapping kit is a surveyor's tape, which is a steel or fiberglass tape thirty or more meters or yards in length. Exact measurements (i.e., for artifact proveniences) can best be obtained with such a tape. Even with a tape, however, the mapper must consider the degree of accuracy of the tape as specified by its manufacturer. The tension at which it is stretched, and the temperature of the tape while the measurement is being made can adversely affect the accuracy of any given tape. Clearly, exact measurements are relatively hard to obtain, although they are possible.

Usually such attention to accuracy is unnecessary. As I have noted previously, the constraints imposed by reducing a map to page size and the physical limitations of drafting itself absorb the error that might result from the differences that tension or temperature have on the tape. Consequently, factors that affect the accuracy of the average tape can be considered inconsequential given the relative degree of accuracy appropriate for most archaeological projects. If your interest is in exact provenience, however, it would be wise to consult with tape manufacturers or suppliers relative to your specific needs.

Barring the above, what kind of surveyor's tape should be purchased? There are three basic set-ups available: the tape enclosed in a case; the tape on a reel; and the utility tape, *sans* case or reel. The tape enclosed in a case is the most common in use on archaeological projects, probably because of availability. A tape such as this can be purchased at any hardware store because it is more rightly a carpenter's tape than a surveyor's tape.

The tape on the reel is the easiest to use of the three. These have large handles and cranks for easy retraction, and are usually cheaper than the encased tape. They are, however, somewhat bulky, but will fit into the main compartment of a backpack.

The utility tape is exactly that: a tape with no reel or case, which is coiled around your arm, like a rope. Lietz makes a 100m version that sells for slightly less than $30.00 (versus $38.00 for a Lufkin 50m tape on a reel and $48.00 for a Lufkin 30m encased tape). Economy and ease of use argue for the purchase of the utility tape. I have found mine to serve satisfactorily for a number of years, and it is much easier to use than any encased tape I have ever encountered.

The third piece of basic mapping equipment is a book of stadia reduction tables. With a Brunton compass, a good tape, and these tables a relatively accurate contour map can be made. Stadia reduction tables provide the correction factor to a horizontal plane for a given ground surface distance at a given vertical angle, and through their use the distance on the ground measured with the tape can be converted to planimetric distance. Books on these tables in North America are usually in the English system; since archaeological projects in this country usually key in to the U.S.G.S. base maps, stadia reduction tables expressed in feet make sense here. The metric system is more elegant from a mathematical standpoint, but it is hard to resist the overwhelming amount of data already available in feet and inches. Note, also, that the stadia reduction table is essential for mapping with a transit, discussed below (see fig. 1).

With the basic mapping kit (Brunton, tape, and stadia reduction tables) archaeological, cultural, and geographical features can be mapped-in, and elevation contours can be determined. For site surveying, preliminary excavations and final excavations at many sites this should be adequate, although a simple line level and string can be added to establish precise elevational changes (for example, to correlate stratigraphic units between excavation units). Yet, the Brunton is only so accurate for vertical and horizontal readings. This becomes important when the site to be mapped is large. In such cases a transit and a stadia rod may be used, but it should be remembered that these tools are more accurate only for measuring the vertical angle of a slope and the horizontal direction, or azimuth, of a feature to be mapped. Consequently, a transit is best used in conjunction with a stadia rod and a tape.

What should be considered in purchasing a transit? Two things are important here: the accuracy necessary, and the approximate size of the sites to be mapped. These two factors are interrelated: the larger the site, the more crucial differences of a few minutes or seconds become in accurately measuring directions. But again, once one begins to draw the map it will be found that protractors graduated to less than 0.5 degrees are rare. Regardless of how accurate you wish to be in the field, you will always be constrained by the mechanical limitations of final draftsmanship.

As of 1982, the average price for a transit is in the vicinity of $1800.00, not including tripod and stadia rod. This, obviously, is a major bite out of any field budget. There are, however, two alternatives to the $1800.00 transit. The first of these is the so-called utility transit, which is essentially a bottom-of-the-line model offered by many manufacturers. Lietz sells a utility transit model (No. 115A) for about $800.00, as does Berger (Model 100N) for around $1000.00, as well as a variety of other companies. These utility transits are generally less accurate than the more highly priced models, and lack some of the luxury features (such as the optical plummet).

Having worked in the field with one of these utility transits (not named above) I can state that they are adequate as regards accuracy for almost all archaeological applications. My only reservation is their quality: they are unabashedly bottom-of-the-line instruments, and I have some doubt about their ability to withstand the use and abuse they would suffer during the average field school. On the other hand, the average transit only gets used by its archaeological proprietor for a short period in any given season, so with some extra caution in handling the utility transit should suffice as a mapping instrument for some time.

The second option is to shift to a lesser instrument, but purchase a top-of-the-line model. By lesser instrument here I mean a builder's level, which is created for obtaining readings on a horizontal plane. Lietz, Berger and David White, however, sell models that are level-transits, which is to say that they are supplied with horizontal and vertical verniers, a magnetic compass, and stadia reticles in the eyepiece. Consequently, these instruments have all the features of the utility transits and comparable degrees of accuracy. Because they are classed as levels, rather than transits, per se, they are substantially cheaper. Additionally, they are somewhat more rugged and better built than the utility transits, in the sense that they are top-of-the-line levels. The David White Model S-8307 can be used at distances of up to 400 feet and retails for just under $500.00; Berger has models costing around $550.00 (Model 504, with an optical plummet) and $435.00 (No. 324); and Lietz supplies a level-transit for $420.00 (Model 200). I use David White S-8307 and I am convinced that it is the perfect instrument for the archaeologist. Its only limitation is the distance factor, but I have found that it is rare that measurements are needed in excess of 100 yards. The David White level-transit is easy to set-up, can be used for readings to 5 minutes, is very rugged and, unlike a transit, once it is leveled does not have to be re-leveled after each reading.

If a transit is to be used a stadia or leveling rod is also required. There are many brands and varieties of these available. Both Mound City and Lietz offer telescoping, fiberglass rods that are quite an improvement over traditional wood or aluminum models. Whoever is assigned the task of holding and carrying the rod will appreciate the lightness and portability of the fiberglass rods. Additionally, although they are somewhat more expensive than the cheapest rods on the market ($80.00 versus $63.00), they are cheaper than both the metal-faced and the aluminum rods, and they will probably hold up as well.

The basic mapping kit, then, is a Brunton compass, a good tape, and a book of stadia reduction tables, for a total cost of less than $200.00. For more complicated, sophisticated or longer mapping jobs a transit and stadia rod can be added. Based on the David White level-transit with a fiberglass rod and a metal tripod, an additional $700.00 can be spent. This total of about $900.00 is half the cost of the average transit yet provides a flexible, rugged, and sufficiently accurate set of mapping tools for archaeological purposes. The kit does not have the luxury features of the $1800.00 transit, but contains everything needed for 99% of all archaeological mapping chores.

Making the Map

I have mentioned earlier that a Brunton, a stadia reduction table and a tape can be used to make a contour map; here I would like to briefly illustrate how this is done. This approach provides a real shortcut to planimetric mapping that is particularly useful for maps quickly made while surveying, for example. The use of the stadia reduction table can also be applied to mapping with a transit and it will be found that this will result in more rapid and accurate map making.

The first procedure in contour mapping with this equipment is to measure the ground surface distance between the mapper at the datum and the feature or point to be mapped. Remember that in terms of making a planimetric map of part of the earth's surface (which, of course, is round) the ground surface distance is the equivalent of the circumference of a sphere. To make a planimetric map we are only really interested in the diameter of the sphere, not its circumference. Hence the groundsurface distance between the datum and the point to be mapped must be reduced to the horizontal distance between the two points, or, their distance apart "as the crow flies."

Reduction to a horizontal plane requires two pieces of information, one of which is the ground surface distance that has been obtained with the surveyor's tape. The other piece of information is the vertical angle off the horizontal plane of the point being mapped relative to the datum; in other words, where the point lies relative to being either above or below the datum/horizontal datum plane. The Brunton can be employed to measure this vertical angle, using the vertical vernier and long-level (or vial level). Complete instructions for taking vertical angles or slope measurements are included with Bruntons and will not be repeated here in detail. Brief-

STADIA REDUCTIONS FOR READING 100					
Vertical Angle	Horizontal Correction	Difference in Elevation	Vertical Angle	Horizontal Correction	Difference in Elevation
2°—00′	0.1	3.5	18°—30′	10.1	30.1
3°—00′	0.3	5.3	19°—00′	10.6	30.8
4°—00′	0.5	7.0	19°—30′	11.2	31.5
5°—00′	0.8	8.7	20°—00′	11.7	32.1
6°—00′	1.1	10.4	20°—30′	12.3	32.8
7°—00′	1.5	12.1	21°—00′	12.8	33.5
8°—00′	1.9	13.8	21°—30′	13.4	34.1
9°—00′	2.5	15.5	22°—00′	14.0	34.7
10°—00′	3.0	17.10	22°—30′	14.7	35.4
10°—30′	3.3	17.9	23°—00′	15.3	36.0
11°—00′	3.6	18.7	23°—30′	15.9	36.6
11°—30′	4.0	19.5	24°—00′	16.5	37.2
12°—00′	4.3	20.3	24°—30′	17.2	37.7
12°—30′	4.7	21.1	25°—00′	17.9	38.3
13°—00′	5.1	21.9	25°—30′	18.6	39.0
13°—30′	5.5	22.7	26°—00′	19.2	39.4
14°—00′	5.9	23.4	26°—30′	19.9	39.9
14°—30′	6.3	24.2	27°—00′	20.6	40.5
15°—00′	6.7	25.0	27°—30′	21.3	41.0
15°—30′	7.2	25.8	28°—00′	22.0	42.0
16°—00′	7.6	26.5	28°—30′	22.8	41.9
16°—30′	8.1	27.2	29°—00′	23.5	42.4
17°—00′	8.5	28.0	29°—30′	24.3	42.9
17°—30′	9.0	28.7	30°—00′	25.0	43.3
18°—00′	9.5	29.4			

Table 1: Stadia reduction tables for selected angles at a 100 foot distance.

ly, however, this procedure involves sighting in the feature, or directly above the feature, at a height equal to your eye height, moving the vertical vernier with the small crank on the back of the compass case until the long-level is horizontal (position the mirror so that you can see when this occurs), and taking the vertical reading from the vernier. Note that the vertical angle off the horizontal plane is not the same thing as the slope between two points. Slope is measured in percent, with 100% slope the equivalent of a 45 degree angle.

For the sake of illustration suppose that we are interested in mapping-in a feature that we have measured and found to be 100 feet from the datum. Using the Brunton we have determined that its vertical angle is –5 degrees. Both of these pieces of information took roughly a few minutes to determine. To place the feature on the map we must determine its planimetric distance from the datum, the difference in elevation between the datum and the point being mapped, and of course the direction of the object from the datum.

A much abbreviated stadia reduction table is presented as Table 1. This table provides the horizontal correction and difference in elevation for selected vertical angles at a distance of 100 feet. Going down the vertical column on the left until the 5 degree row is located, it can be seen that 100 feet of ground surface should be reduced 0.8 feet for the planimetric or horizontal distance, and that the difference in elevation between the datum and the feature is 8.7 feet. Since our vertical angle is negative (i.e. down as opposed to up), this difference in elevation is also negative. Hence, the feature should be plotted on the map as 99.2 feet from the datum and 8.7 feet lower than the datum. The Brunton can of course also be used to take the azimuthal direction of the feature from the datum.

A complete contour map can be made following this procedure. In the sense that a tape is more accurate than a transit and stadia rod for measuring ground surface distances, this contour map can actually be more accurate than many transit/stadia maps. Additionally, it should be obvious from the above example that horizontal reduction factors are usually small; so small, in fact, that they often cannot be shown on the final map given the scale at which it is usually drawn. This argues for the notion of the Brunton, although less exact than a transit for taking vertical angles, can provide adequate readings of the vertical angle when distance measures are the primary concern. On the other hand, the transit will allow you to more accurately measure this vertical angle and thereby give you a better determination of the difference in elevation between any two points. For most archaeological applications, however, the Brunton, tape and stadia reduction tables provide an accuracy that is completely adequate, particularly when the generalization that is required for reduction of the map to an 8½ by 11 inch size is considered.

The stadia reduction tables can also of course be used for reducing data derived from a transit and stadia rod or, more preferably, a transit, rod and tape. The tables will greatly accelerate the speed at which the final map is made, and by using them your accuracy will be equal to that of most civil engineers.

Conclusion

Mapping archaeological sites, in summary, is not a particularly difficult task although it is sometimes tedious and is too often relegated to someone that is ill-prepared to do an adequate job. The most important thing that an archaeologist can do to prepare for this task is to determine what the accuracy needs are for the specific job in question, and then to choose the proper equipment in order to meet that level of accuracy. Mapping in the exact provenience of artifacts, for example, is a relatively difficult task that sometimes cannot be achieved with a transit and stadia rod alone. On the other hand, the mapping of most sites can be handled using simple equipment such as a Brunton compass, a surveyor's tape, and a stadia reduction table. Given the size of most archaeological maps in their published form and the amount of generalization that is required for maps of such scale, these tools can be used to obtain mapping data that are sufficiently accurate for most archaeological purposes, and in certain cases, will be more accurate than maps make with more sophisticated and expensive equipment.

Author's Notes

I have noted earlier that encased tapes are most commonly used, largely because they are the most readily available. Where, then, can tapes on reels, stadia reduction tables and the like be obtained? Some building supply yards handle surveying equipment, if they have a hardware section. Most large cities have stores that specialize in surveying supplies (look under "Surveying instruments" in the yellow pages of the phone book). Lacking access to a big city, the final alternative is mail order. I recommend the Ben Meadows Company for postal shopping (P.O. Box 2781, Eugene, Oregon, 97402 or 3589 Broad St., Atlanta (Chamblee), Georgia, 30366). They are relatively fast, they provide a complete catalog with prices, and they guarantee what they sell. The prices that I have quoted above were obtained from the 14th edition of their general catalog.

A METHOD FOR EFFECTIVELY SCREENING SOME CLAY MATRICES

David M. Van Horn and John R. Murray

Introduction

This paper reports on a new archaeological field technique developed during the excavation of a portion of a prehistoric quarry site located in the foothills of the Santa Ana Mountains. The site, which has been designated Ora-507, is characterized in part by a very pure clay matrix which contains quantities of chipped stone cores and debitage (Van Horn and Murray, n.d.). The purpose of this article is to describe the method which we used to efficiently screen the clay in order to recover the flaked stone.

Initial testing at Ora-507 was conducted in 1977 under the supervision of Roger J. Desautels (SP.S N.D.). Testing was performed by digging a series of backhoe trenches and excavating 30-centimeter-square column samples fromfrom the walls of the trenches. Excavation was extremely difficult in portions of the site because of the matrix which comprises a very pure, greasy, black clay. We later learned that this soil is known to geologists as Bosanko clay. It is described as follows:

> ... dark gray (10YR 4/1) clay, black (10YR 2/1) [when]
> moist; moderate very coarse prismatic structure; extremely
> hard, firm, very sticky and very plastic... mildly alkaline
> ...(Watchell 1978:15).

The clay has such extraordinary adhesive and plastic qualities that conventional screening techniques are rendered useless. Dry screening was of no avail whatsoever and several days were required to hydraulically screen two 30 x 30 centimeter column samples. It became clear that prohibitive time and expense would be entailed in attempting to screen a substantial quantity of the clay using conventional methods.

Development of the Method

We investigated possible alternatives to screening by contacting an individual who was experienced in clay quarrying, and were told that mechanical means were normally used for mining clays but that sodium carbonate (Na_2CO_3) had been used at times. This led us to contact several individuals who had some familiarity with soil chemistry (K. D. Bergin, pers. comm.; R. Schafer, pers. comm.). Clays are composed of particles that are less than 5 microns in their maximum dimension and which are frequently almost totally impermeable to plain water because the spaces between the clay particles are hardly larger than a water molecule. Furthermore, many clays derive their adhesive character from a delicately balanced network of electrical charges carried by the clay particles. The particular clay we were dealing with was probably a montmorillonite which characteristically consists of thin sheets of silica and aluminum bound together by calcium ions (Ca^+; C. Sterling, pers. comm.). In order to eliminate the adhesive property of the clay, it is necessary to introduce an ion which will replace the Ca^+. It was thought that sodium carbonate might achieve this end by introducing a sodium ion (Na^{++}) which would replace the calcium ion.

There are many other known chemical means for accomplishing this result but these are normally intended for laboratory use and entail handling hazardous and/or expensive chemicals. All of the individuals with whom we consulted recommended practical experiment with sodium carbonate and various common household chemicals (bleaches, detergents, etc.) in order to determine which, if any, might work best.

Consequently, we collected a sample of the clay from Ora-507 and returned to the laboratory. We had no sodium carbonate on hand but Mr. Bergin informed us that sodium bicarbonate ($NaHCO_3$; household baking soda) would do as well. At first, we simply immersed one lump of the clay in a bowl of ordinary tap water and another in a bowl of sodium bicarbonate solution. Bubbles appeared on the surface of the clay immersed in the solution and within a few minutes, the lump began to "disintegrate" with no agitation. The lump in the plain water remained unchanged. This initial success led us to attempt to duplicate an actual field situation on a laboratory scale.

Some sort of tank would clearly be required to treat the clay in the field. We planned to use 55-gallon drums cut in half lengthwise, thereby forming two "tanks," estimating that the capacity of each tank would equal 27.5 gallons, less 2.5 gallons of freeboard for each. We calculated that we could process one-half of a 10-centimeter level of a 1 x 1 meter unit in a single tank. Reducing these volumes to a convenient laboratory scale, we calculated that a single cube of clay measuring 8.4 centimeters on a side was to 1 liter of water as 25 gallons is to 0.5 of a 10-centimeter level from a 1-meter square excavation unit. The cube was formed, cut up, and placed in 1 liter of water mixed with 20 gm of $NaHCO_3$ (fig. 1). Agitation of any kind was carefully avoided. After ten minutes, the clay had visibly deteriorated and after four hours, it had deteriorated completely.

Various further experiments were subsequently conducted, one of which entailed substitution of sodium carbonate for sodium bicarbonate (the former being somewhat less expensive), and the use of de-ionized water. Addition of various readily available household chemicals including ammonia, hydrogen peroxide, chlorine bleaches, boron compounds, and phosphate containing detergents were all tried with no improvements over the results of the initial experiment. We were somewhat surprised that the sodium carbonate did not work as well as the bicarbonate and later consulted Mr. Sterling (pers. comm.) who suggested that the carbon dioxide bubbles were forming a mild carbonic acid (H_2CO_3) in the solution (we shall return to this subject later). Additional experiments showed that the rate of clay disintegration seemed to be directly proportional to the density of the sodium bicarbonate solution. Consequently, a saturated solution was used in the field (approximately 80 gm of $NaHCO_3$ per liter of water).

Initial Field Application

Construction of the equipment for processing the clay was a relatively simple matter. We discovered that 33-gallon drums were much less expensive and more readily available at local wrecking yards; therefore, a series of these were purchased and cut lengthwise with an acetylene torch. A cardboard template of the vertical cross-section of the tank was then used for the construction of 3/4-inch plywood ends for the screen frames (fig. 2). The ends were cut so that there would be about two inches of clearance between the bottom of the screen and the bottom of the tank in order to permit broken down clay to build up after passing through the mesh. The remainder of the screen frame was then built from 2 x 2 and I x 2 inch stock as shown in the illustration. One-eighth-inch galvanized steel mesh was then stapled to the screen frame. The completed screens fit into the tanks so that clay from the excavation units could be placed in the screens to soak in the solution.

Slightly over 3 cubic meters of clay were screened in the field using the bicarbonate solution. We discovered than an entire 10-centimeter level from a 1-meter square excavation unit could be placed in from six to eight tanks depending upon the amount of clay placed in each. The solution causes carbon dioxide bubles to be given off when it is working well (fig. 3). It completely broke down the purest clay in approximately forty minutes with no agitation, though we found that stirring with a wooden paddled constructed for this purpose increased the speed of the process. We also found that it was useful to break the clay into small (approximately 10 cm) lumps before immersion in order to expose more surface area.

Once the clay was broken down, it left a wet, sandy mud in the bottom of the screen. The screen was then removed and placed at a tilt against the side of the tank (fig. 3b). The muddy residue could be sprayed through the mesh in a matter of seconds using water under standard pressure from a garden hose fitted with a spray nozzle. The artifacts remaining in the screen were cleaned and then simply removed for drying. While an entire 10 centimeter level could be processed over a forty minute period, we found that a two-man team working a single unit required only four tanks to keep busy with the digging and screening.

We also found that the bicarbonate solution could be used repeatedly with no loss in its effectiveness. In fact, the solution seemed to improve with use and this was the subject of much speculation and an occasional facetious remark. We now believe that Mr. Sterling's hypothesis regarding formation of a mild carbonic acid in the tank is probably correct. Each time a new load of clay is placed in a tank, additional carbon dioxide bubbles through the solution, thus strengthening its carbonic acid content. In any event, two or three inches of sludge formed in the bottom of each tank after processing three or four loads and this was simply shoveled out, taking care to lose as little of the solution as possible.

Use of the bicarbonate solution permitted 100 percent recovery of all solid objects larger than 1/8-inch in their minimum dimension. In fact, the method proved so effective that we have since tried it at two other archaeological sites.

Subsequent Field Applications

In 1980, CA-Ora-839, a coastal shell midden on a bluff overlooking the Santa Ana River near Newport Beach, was archaeologically tested. The midden contained little clay and required only plain water to screen. However, under the midden we encountered a very hard red clay which appeared totally unlike the clay at Ora-507. We were uncertain as to whether this clay contained cultural material though none was evident. In order to make certain, we excavated into the clay using the bicarbonate soaking solution to screen the backdirt.

The solution worked very well and resulted in the recovery of an entirely new pre-shell midden phase of the site. Cultural material extended into the red clay stratum to a depth in excess of one meter below the shell midden. It is unlikely that any cultural material whatsoever would have been recovered using conventional screening techniques. This is because the finds in the clay were restricted to pressure flakes and occasional small fish vertebrae which would probably not have been found were 100 percent of the excavated clay not screened using the new system.

A second application of the bicarbonate screening solution was carried out this year at LAn-669, a late prehistoric inland campsite in the Conejo Valley next to the Los Angeles/Ventura County line. Here the clay resembled the montmorillonite type familiar from Ora-507. The only problem was that there was no pressurized water supply anywhere near the site. In the past, we had had obtained water by using up to 2,500 feet of the 3/4-inch garden hose. However, even this length was inadequate to bring water in at LAn-669. Adequate volumes of water under pressure (approximately 20 lb./inch^2 at minimum) are absolutely essential to the effective use of the screening solution.

Mr. Sterling suggested that we use a water truck, and he arranged to rent such a vehicle fitted with an 1,100 gallon tank from a local equipment rental firm (fig. 4). We also requested that the local water district place a meter on the nearest fire hydrant which was less than a mile away. The water truck was then filled from the hydrant using a 1.5 inch fire hose (hydrant meters normally have a 3-inch outlet, and it is necessary to rent an adapter to break the outlet size down to the hose connection size). The hydrant supplied sufficient water to fill the truck in approximately twenty minutes; the truck was then driven to the site.

Water was removed from the truck by connecting its 1.5 inch outlet to a portable three horsepower centrifugal water pump using 1.5 inch plastic irrigation hose. The system is self-priming since opening the valve on the water truck outlet permits water to fill the impeller housing of the pump. The discharge outlet of the pump (1.5 inches) was broken down to a garden hose connection using a series of PVC plastic pipe connections, and the opposite end of the garden hose was fitted with a trigger-type nozzle so that the operator could spray at will. The pump can be left running at all times, regardless of whether the water is being used. We found that the truck would supply about one day's worth of water for a 1 x 1 meter excavation unit. Water pressure was more than adequate to drive the sludge from the screens in two or three minutes, leaving the contents of the screen clean.

A: 8.4 cm. cube of clay.

B: Cube after being cut up and immersed in the NaHCO$_3$ solution.

C: Break-down after 10 minutes.

D: Break-down after four hours.

Figure 1: The initial experiment. Clay from Ora-507 is chemically broken down.

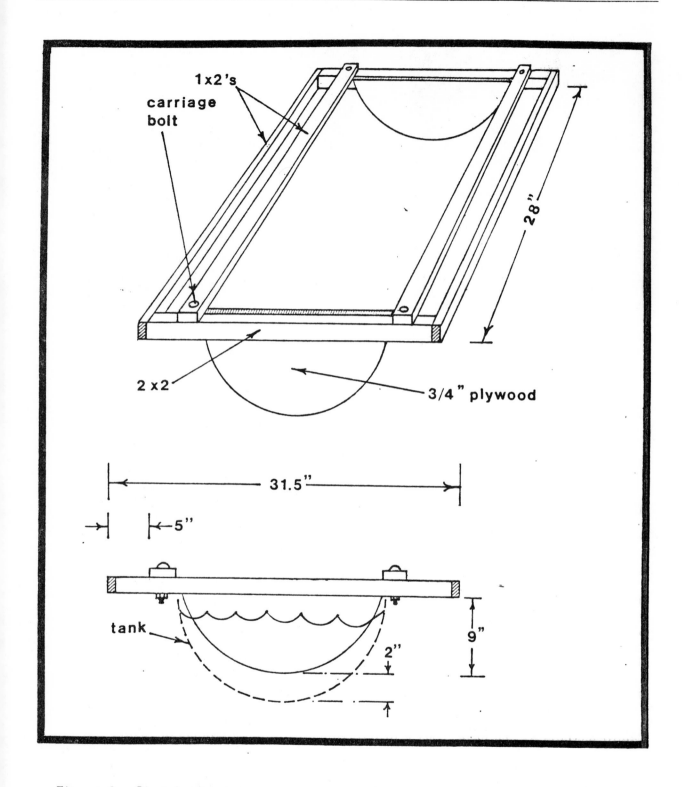

Figure 2: Sketch showing screen construction. 33 gallon drum dimensions will vary somewhat, so use caution in cutting and measuring.

Figure 3:   The process in use in an archaeological field context.

One unit was to be placed near a spring. This area was inaccessible by water truck at the time of our excavations and we did not have a sufficiently long section of irrigation hose to reach the spring area from the dirt road used by the truck. Consequently, we set up a smaller (2.5 h.p.) centrifugal pump fitted with a sump next to the spring. A hole was dug for the sump and this provided a reservoir in which the spring water could collect. The discharge outlet of the pump was fitted with a garden hose as described above. At first we tried spraying plain water at soil in a standard shaker screen but this system failed due to the adhesiveness of the wet soil. Therefore, a series of bicarbonate tanks were set up and worked well, and an excellent degree of recovery was obtained.

While all of this equipment may sound somewhat elaborate to the reader, we found that everything was quite portable and easy to use; in fact, all of the equipment was packed up and removed many miles from the site each night.

Drawbacks to the Bicarbonate Screening Method

While we are pleased with the practical utility of the bicarbonate solution screening method, it does nevertheless suffer from some disadvantages and these should be pointed out. First, the system leaves the excavator without dirt for backfilling his excavation. We have overcome this problem by obtaining fill elsewhere and transporting it to the site in a small pickup truck.

Secondly, the process apparently removes the calcium from the soil. The residual sludge is also quite fine-grained and dries in hard sheets. These observations may account for the fact that plants do not grow well in soils that have undergone the screeening process, and the problem may be overcome by careful selection of the screening location in advance of the actual work.

An additional problem is that the effects of the process upon potential carbon

Figure 4: Views of the bicarbonate screening method using a portable water tank truck, and gas-operated centrifugal pump in the field.

samples are presently unknown. One of us discussed this matter with Mr. P. Stota of the University of California, Riverside, radiocarbon laboratory (personal communication) and after consideration Mr. Stota suggested that the solution would probably not adversely affect organic carbon compounds characteristic of such materials as wood, charcoal, and bone. On the other hand, the carbonic acid in the solution would affect inorganic carbonates such as are found in marine shell. However, there is some question as to whether even this chemical action would adversely affect the sample since such carbonates are normally removed from the sample prior to C-14 analysis. Clearly, some practical experiment is called for in order to resolve the question with a degree of certainty.

Finally, and most important, it is not known whether the solution will work efficiently on all clay soils. Our experiments have been restricted to coastal southern California clays and we have no basis for judging how effective the bicarbonate solution would be in treating clays elsewhere. Fortunately, the problem is easily resolved since an investigator need only obtain a sample of the soil from the prospective site and then place it in a bowl of water and baking soda.

Costs

The cost of using the bicarbonate solution screening process is low once the most basic equipment has been built. Steel drums can be easily purchased from local scrap yards for a marginal cost (approx. $5.00/drum). The raw materials for constructing the screens cost less than $10.00 per screen, although construction may take several hours per frame and a minumum of four would be required to excavate a single 1 x 1 meter unit. Sodium bicarbonate is available in 100-pound bags from industrial chemical supply outlets. At present, a bag costs approximately $30.00 and should supply sufficient solution to process about 1 cubic meter of clay. If a water source is available, these items are all that are needed except for a 3/4-inch garden hose and spray nozzle.

If water is not available, the process becomes somewhat more expensive. A water truck of the type described above rents for about $100.00 per day and the operator must supply his own water. A centrifugal water pump costs about $200.00 though once purchased, it will be available for future use. Gasoline and pipe fittings also add to the additional cost.

Conclusion

Use of the bicarbonate solution on appropriate clays permits 100 percent recovery of all solid objects of any size, depending upon the mesh size of the screens. The solution is non-toxic and presents no hazard to the safety of the excavation staff. The process is relatively inexpensive and can be performed by anyone with readily available materials. It is so effective that in one instance, it has enabled us to find cultural material in a clay matrix where none was visible and where it is unlikely that any would have been found using conventional screening techniques. However, its effects on C-14 samples are not presently known, and the bicarbonate solution may not be effective in breaking down all clays.

Acknowledgments

We wish to thank the Environmental Management Agency (EMA) of the County of Orange for sponsoring our first application of the bicarbonate screening process at Ora-507, and are particularly grateful to Mr. Rob Selway of the EMA for his assistance and encouragement. Professor Riley Schafer (University of Wyoming) also offered much helpful advice. Mr. Kieran D. Bergin, a chemical engineer with the County of Los Angeles, was of invaluable assistance. Finally, Mr. Cecil Sterling (Ultrasystems, Inc.) discovered how to get a water supply at LAn-669 and made other valuable suggestions with regard to the chemical phenomena taking place within the tanks.

X RAYS IN ARCHAEOLOGICAL ANALYSIS

Louis J. Tartaglia

Introduction

A relatively accessible and inexpensive technique that can be adapted to archaeological laboratory analysis involves the examination of both artifacts and osteological materials with X-rays. Physical archaeologists have long appreciated the information value of x-rays and x-ray photography, and in some cases Old World archaeologists have used the technique to great advantage. This paper relates the practical application of X-rays in two separate archaeological contexts from the New World; the results in both cases were the discovery of cultural and/or physical anomalies that would not normally be visible to the unaided vision of the analyst. One study reconstructs South American (Moche and Chimu) ceramic technology while the other examines social stratification at the Medea Creek cemetery in California as suggested by radiopaque transverse (or Harris') lines.

Many problems are involved in the detailed reconstruction of ceramic technology. Both Chimu and Moche ceramic vessels were experimentally subjected to radiographic analysis in an attempt to resolve specific questions about manufacturing processes, and the results produced evidence for the fabrication procedure originally advanced by Donnan (1965) as the means by which Moche stirrup-spout vessels were created. The analysis also identified certain characteristics which have not been previously recorded and which may represent distinguishable evidence for different and identifiable ceramic workshops.

Radiopaque transverse lines were counted on X-rays to determine their frequency variability of occurrence in femora (distal end) and tibiae (proximal end) from a Late Horizon prehistoric California Indian population, and significant statistical correlations were obtained. By examining and analyzing the relative frequency of transverse lines in association with mortuary practices (burial goods, grave pit depth), social stratification within the Medea Creek cemetery could be partially reconstructed.

X-rays and Prehistoric Ceramic Technology

The production of Moche ceramics utilizes four basic techniques: coiling, molding, modelling and stamping; however, most vessels are not made by a single method but in fact represent the end products of combinations of at least two or more. In many cases, since "all traces of fabrication were removed in the finishing process" (Donnan, 1965: 118), it is very difficult to determine which construction processes were used for particular vessels. Manufacturing marks often remain on vessel interiors, and are easily identified from sherds or partially broken vessels, but closed and complete vessel forms provide little opportunity to study production techniques; therefore, conclusions about their stages of manufacture are often speculative.

Donnan's (ibid) experimental analysis has suggested a set of sequential steps in the production of stirrup spout vessels; these are outlined in graphic form in Figures 1 through 18. While most students of prehistoric ceramic technology accept Donnan's reconstruction, all would agree that additional evidence of material nature would reinforce his thesis. X-ray photographic analysis has provided evidence in practical support of Donnan's reconstruction.

Methods

X-ray photographic analysis was conducted on two stirrup spout vessels in order to determine the capabilities, limitations, and future applicability of radiographs in reconstructing prehistoric ceramic technology. In the interests of obtaining the maximum resolution possible, it is recommended that the archaeologist be present when the technician X-rays any ceramic vessel. If necessary, mercury can be siphoned into a stirrup spout vessel so as to enhance the visibility of manufacturing details.

Ansco cronex 6 medical film was used in association with a 300 milliamp small focal spot Westinghouse rotating anode machine. The exposures were taken at 1/60th of a second for top views and for 1/30th of a second for cross sections. The focal distance for all radiographs was 183 centimeters; the line voltage and filament power were maintained at 120 kilovolts. All films were developed by an automatic Pako processor in 90 seconds.

Moche Ceramic Reconstruction

According to Donnan (1965: 122-124), the manufacturing technique involved in Moche stirrup spout vessel reconstruction is the following. The main chamber of the vessel is partly formed in a two piece mold (Figures 1, 2, & 3). An opening is left at the top of the chamber which enables the potter to smooth the interior surface.

When the clay in the mold is dry and firm, the chamber is removed from the mold. After the lower part of the chamber is dry, the upper portion is finished by a coiling technique (Figure 4). It is noted that coiling is used in conjunction with molding to produce a particular Moche vessel form (Donnan ibid:119). The remnants of the distinct coils are clearly visible on the interior portion of the molded chamber in the radiograph (Figure 19) but all external evidence of the coils has been completely removed. This indicates that a coiling technique was probably used in forming the upper chamber of the vessel, which is not discernible to the unaided eye by any external surface examination. However, an alternative explanation of this recorded anomaly is that these apparent coils may represent finger wipe marks as a by-

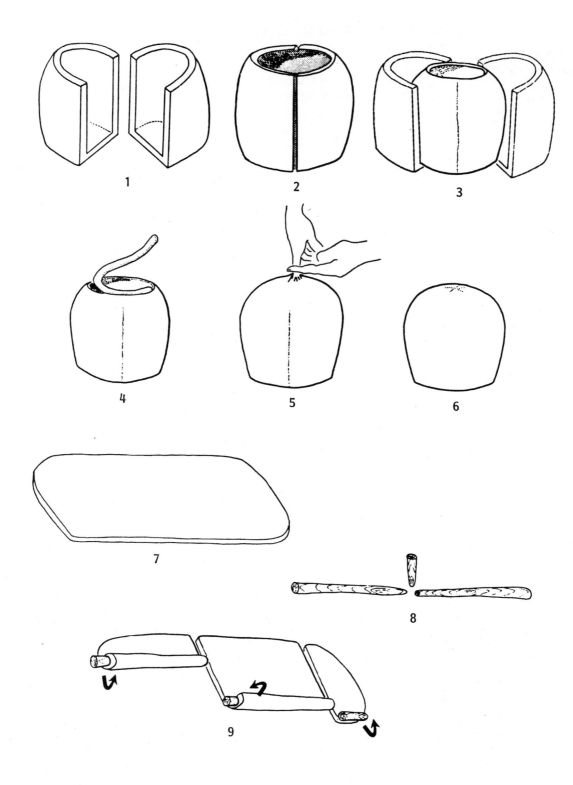

Figures 1 through 9: Steps in the construction of a stirrup spout vessel. The body is formed with the use of a two-part mold (Figures 1-6), and the spout is shaped over jigs in sections (Figures 7-9). Reprinted from Donnan, 1965: Plate II, courtesy of the Institute of Andean Studies.

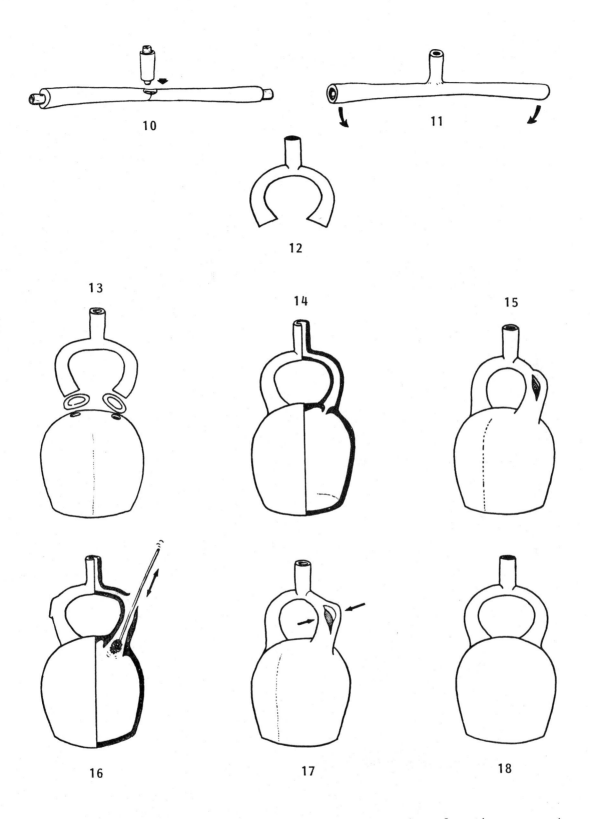

Figures 10 through 18: Final steps in construction of a stirrup spout vessel. Completion of the spout (Figures 10–12) and joining the spout to the body (Figures 13–18). Reprinted from Donnan, 1965: Plate III, courtesy of the Institute of Andean Studies.

product of adhering clay to the inner surface of a press mold; both interpretations are viable although the former one appears to be more plausible.

Next, a small opening remains in the chamber, and it is sealed (Figures 5 & 6). The stirrup spout is manufactured by the following procedure. A thin sheet of clay is cut into wide strips (Figure 7), which are wrapped around three tapered wooden rods (Figures 8 & 9). The resulting seams are then sealed and joined together at their small ends. The seam junctions are smoothed and reinforced by a small clay ring which is placed into the joint (Figure 10). The wooden rods are now removed, and the remaining two clay tubes are bent to form the hoop of the stirrup spout (Figures 11 & 12). The spout is now allowed to become firm, but not dry (Donnan ibid:123). Remains of this process appear on a radiograph (Figure 20) which reveal both junction seams at the neck of the vessel, and a clearly indicated gradual decrease in the width of both the neck and the spout by the use of the tapered wooden rods.

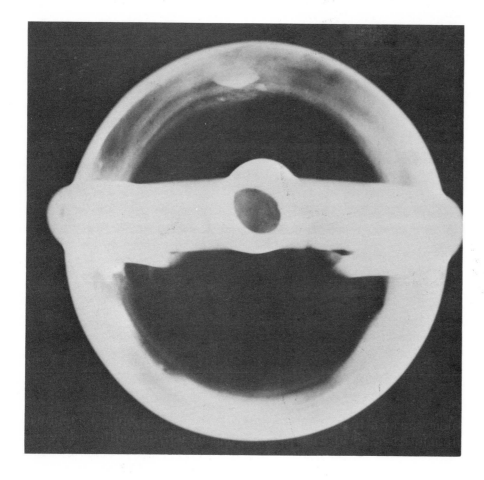

Figure 19: Top view of stirrup spout vessel with manufacturing marks (coiling) visible on its interior.

The stirrup spout is joined to the chamber by punching two holes in the chamber where the stirrup spout is to be attached with the aid of a small clay coil wrapped around each joint (Figure 13). These coils (Figure 14) are subsequently smoothed into the joints and reinforce them (Donnan, ibid).

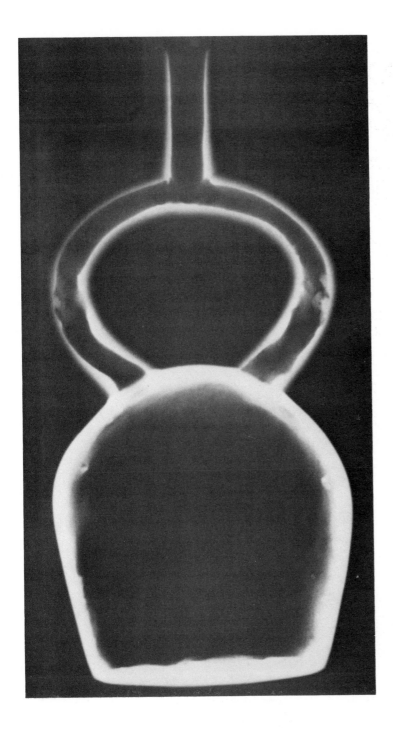

Figure 20: Side view of a Moche stirrup spout vessel. Note the joint marks at top, indicating that the stirrup was created through the attachment of three separate sections. Also note the remnant holes (smoothed over) at the point of greatest outcurvature on either side of the stirrup; these provide evidence for the use of a swab stick to seal the spout interior to the body. UCLA Museum of Culture History X65-8713.

Next, a small vertical slit is made in the shoulder of the spout and is opened (Figure 15). A swab stick is now inserted into the opening and used to ream out the inner trough of the spout at the chamber junction (Figure 16). The swab is then removed and the spout is pressed back into its original shape (Figures 17 & 18). All external traces of these vertical slits are eventually removed. Radiographic cross-sections of stirrup spouts reveal vestiges of reamer slits and inner ridges of clay as a by-product of this process on the inner portion of the spout shoulder (Figures 20 & 21). A distinct mold seam on the Chimu stirrup spout was detected in a separate radiograph from above and indicates that this vessel's spout

Figure 21: Side view of a Chimu stirrup spout vessel made by a different technique than that shown in Figure 20. Note the differences in the wall thickness of the spout, and in the care with which joints are made. UCLA Museum of Culture History, X68-1002.

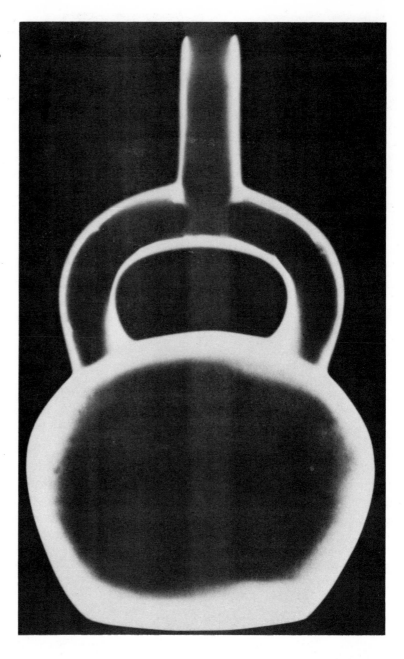

was molded separately and subsequently joined to the chamber; the stirrup spout is not molded integrally with the chamber.

The quality control of ceramic production of stirrup spouts and their associated manufacturing stages (e.g. vestiges of reamer slits in the spout shoulder, a constant internal thickness of the cross section of the spout, etc.) are evident (compare Figures 20 & 21). A tremendous difference in the dexterity and skill of presumably two separate artisans is apparent by studying the radiographs of these two vessels. By observing the chamber and spout manufacturing stages of stirrup spout vessels, it is posited that distinct differences in construction relate to specific prehistoric ceramic workshops; however, a larger sample would be is required before any conclusions about technologically identifiable prehistoric ceramic workshops can be accepted.

X-rays and Archaeo-osteological Material

Radiopaque transverse lines (or Harris' lines, also called arrested growth lines or bone scars) occur in human long bones as the result of extremely heavy calcification which is triggered by arrested or accelerated bone growth. Such anomalies can result from periods of illness, or from acute malnutrition and/or dietary deficiencies. It has been statistically shown that chronically undernourished children have a higher incidence of scarring (transverse lines) when ethnically identical children are compared (Dreizen, et al., 1964). Moreover, transverse lines develop when a growing animal or human is subjected to periods of stress (such as that which normally accompanies fever) or pressure to a sufficient degree (Caffey, 1967). Transverse lines have in fact been induced in animals by starvation (Harris, 1931). According to Harris (ibid), the generation of arrested growth lines follows certain postulates:

1. The density of the line is proportional to the degree of severity or acuteness of the illness.

2. Lines of arrested growth are manifested more rapidly at the growing ends of the long bones. Caffey (1967) stated that the thickest and widest transverse lines appear at the end of the shaft while older lines, deeper in the shaft, are thinner, less distinct, and usually discontinuous.

3. Lines of arrested growth undergo obliteration as a part of that process of absorption and deposition which is an active feature of the living bone. It has been observed that radiopaque lines record events that transpired in childhood rather than ossified evidence of adolescent stresses (Garn and Schwager 1967).

This study was designed to make use of photographic (X-ray) techniques to ascertain the variability in the frequency of transverse lines in long bones in a prehistoric population and to subsequently correlate observable patterns with social stratification. The procedures employed consisted of counting and analyzing transverse lines in the femur (distal end) and the tibia (proximal/distal ends) that appeared on X-rays taken of eight adult prehistoric California Indians from Medea Creek, a Late Horizon (Ca. A.D. 1500) inland Chumash Indian cemetery with an extremely short time depth (350 years).

Methods

The Medea Creek cemetery (LAn-243) is located near Agoura, California, in the Santa Monica Mountains (L. King 1969). One hundred and seventy six burials were examined to locate complete sets of tibiae and femora from the same individual and respective side for this comparative study. The proximal and distal ends of the tibiae as well as the distal end of the femora were X-rayed to determine the frequency of transverse lines for each bone. Broken and diseased bones were excluded from this statistical study.

Both the age at death and sex of each individual had been previously recorded on the burial record forms from the site; each burial, however, was re-checked for the puposes of this study. Dentition and bone fusion were used for aging while sex was determined from innominate bones when available as well as additional diagnostic features discussed by Brothwell (1965).

Ansco cronex 6 film was used in a 100 milliamp small focal spot Westinghouse rotating anode machine; the exposures were taken at one second at a distance of 102 centimeters. The line voltage and filament were maintained at 60 kilovolts. All films were developed by an automatic Pako processor in 90 seconds. Radiologists at the UCLA Medical Center were consulted so as to accurately determine the number of Harris' lines recorded on each radiograph. The criteria employed for determining this number were maintaining a count of all lines which were transverse to the long bone axis as well as any remnants of such lines that may have been resorbed during adulthood. Whenever possible, all bones were X-rayed in an anterior-posterior position.

Results

The distal end of the femur usually contained the highest frequency of transverse lines, followed in succession by the proximal and distal ends of the tibia. The number of transverse lines and age/sex characteristics of each individual studied are documented in Table 1. The greatest variability in terms of the frequency of transverse lines occurs in the proximal ends of the tibiae; no apparent sex differentiation seems to be evident. It has been noticed that there is no significant sex variation in the age-related pattern frequencies of transverse lines (Dreizen, et al, 1964). Radiographic data revealed that there seems to be no variability evident between age at death and the frequency of transverse lines in long bones in the Medea Creek prehistoric Indian (adult) population, as noted in Table 1.

MEDEA CREEK CEMETERY DATA

BURIAL NUMBER	AGE	SEX	BURIAL LOCATION*	GRAVE GOODS**	STATUS	GRAVE DEPTH***	GRAVE PIT DEPTH	TRANSVERSE LINES		
								Tibia (dist)	Tibia (prox)	Femur (dist)
494- 63	30	M	E-2	0	Low	87	–	–	3	3
494- 94	30	F	E-3	3	Low	87	–	4	9	4
494-107	35	M	E-2	1	Low	122	31	1	6	2
494-403	20-25	M	E-1	0	Low	78	50	12	3	9
494-214	30	F	W-2	126	High	147	73	–	0	5
494-342	23-30	F	E-3	9	High	115	70	0	2	0
494-351	23-30	M	E-3	19	High	140	70	0	0	1
494-352	25-35	M	E-3	4	High	149	89	1	0	0

(*) Burial locations according to L. King, 1969.
(**) Grave goods totals simply indicate the number of artifacts associated with each burial.
(***) Grave depth in this case is below datum. Both these figures and those for grave pit depth are expressed in cm.

Table 1:
Transverse lines in the Medea Creek cemetery population.

Discussion

The highest frequency of transverse lines X-rayed from the prehistoric population at Medea Creek appeared in the distal end of the femur, followed by the proximal and distal ends of the tibia. This concurs with McHenry's study (1968) but other studies (Wells 1961; Gray 1967) noticed that lines of arrested growth are most common in the distal end of the tibia. Consequently, it is apparent that a great deal of variability and fluctuation exists in the frequency of transverse lines between prehistoric populations. Therefore, individual populations must be first considered as separate entities and then compared with contemporary sites on a generalized basis. Also, due to the frequency variability of arrested growth lines pres-

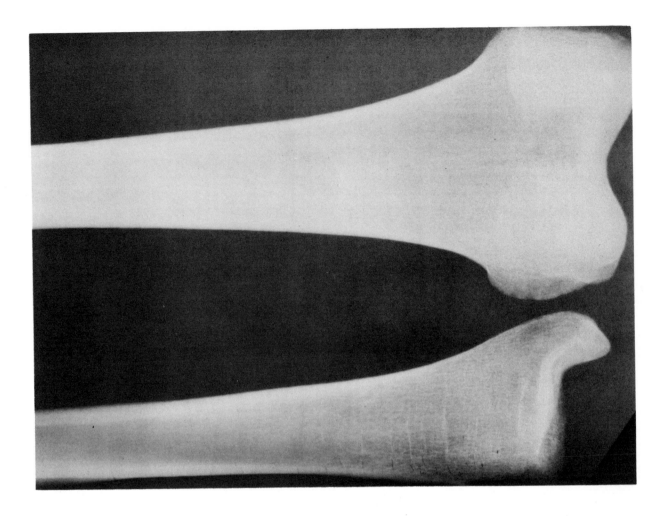

Figure 22: Transverse lines on long bones from a low-status burial (number 403) from Medea Creek cemetery, California.

ent at Medea Creek, it appears that transverse lines in long bones cannot be significantly correlated with distinct archaeological horizons as inferred by McHenry's study (1968) of prehistoric California Indian horizons.

By examining and recording the frequency of transverse lines at Medea Creek, inferences about social stratification (status) at a prehistoric cemetery can be advanced. Status among the Chumash can defined as wealth which is acquired by inheritance; thus, socio-economic stratification existed within villages and extended to cemeteries. Also, rank order of status is associated with specialized individuals within the community, such as chiefs, shamans, and village officials.

The chief acted as headman among the villagers and retained his power (wealth) and social rank order, since he constantly received gifts of food and shell money from villagers (Kroeber, 1925). Furthermore, one's social position was carefully regulated within the community, since high status individuals were paid for their services. For instance, although only rich men owned canoes, they did not participate in the physical activity of catching fish; the catch was their personal

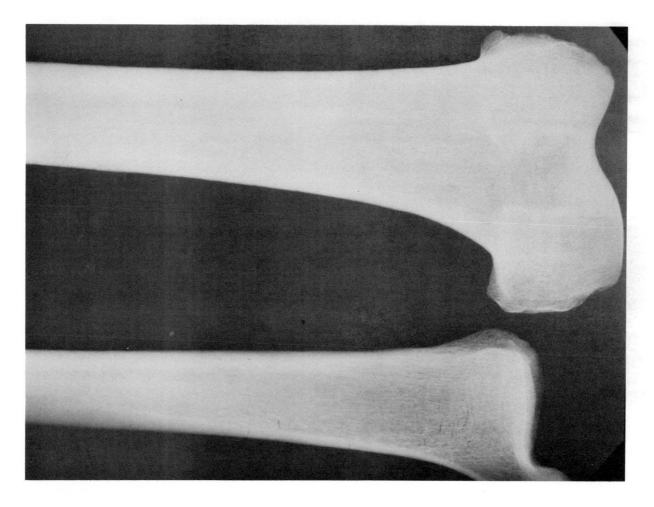

Figure 23: General absence of transverse lines on long bones from a high-status burial (number 352) from the Medea Creek cemetery.

property and distributed accordingly. Among the Ventureno, Harrington recorded a kinship term that applied to the dynasty of nobility. He stated that there were "people who enjoyed special privileges and who had to make no effort to live, it was all provided for them" (L. King, 1969: 45).

Since social status among the Chumash was inherited, individuals of lower social standing were probably subjected to greater environmental stress and pressures than were the elite, hence, they were more susceptible to prolonged periods of stress, acute malnutrition and disease. Considering the historic and ethnographic accounts that have been presented, the following hypothesis may be advanced: individuals of lower social standing in a hunting and gathering society are subjected to greater environmental stress; therefore, people of lower social status will develop a higher incidence of Harris' lines, and social status within a cemetery may be reflected in the frequency of these transverse lines present between individuals.

In order to test this hypothesis, status was determined at Medea Creek by:

1. the relative number of associated burial offerings.

2. the depth of the burial pit.
3. the age of the individual at death.
4. the sex of the burial.

This approach resulted in high and low status categories. The Medea Creek cemetery has been divided into two main sections, the east and west section, separated by an area where burials are absent (ibid).

Another important social factor to be considered in this study is that the Chumash Indians of Southern California had specialized paid grave diggers. Ethnographic and archaeological evidence seems to indicate that deep grave pits were related to high status individuals (ibid). The burials in the eastern area (sections one to three) at Medea Creek have similar depth ranges; however, the western area (section four) has a shallower depth range. Analysis of the burial records from Medea Creek revealed that burials recorded at relatively moderate to shallow depths contained few if any associated grave goods while a higher frequency of burial offerings were encountered at greater depths; consequently, it appears that the relative depth of a grave pit is associated with status (Table 1).

In order to determine social stratification at the Medea Creek cemetery by means of radiopaque transverse lines, all data were statistically analyzed; the UCLA BMD-P2R stepwise regression program was employed. Analysis revealed a strong negative correlation between lines of arrested growth and associated burial goods. This correlation is expected, since individuals of higher status should possess fewer numbers of Harris's lines when compared with individuals of lower status.

For example, a radiograph of a low status burial (number 403) had a total of 24 transverse lines (distal end of the femur and both the distal and proximal ends of the tibia) and no associated artifacts (Figure 22). This burial was located in the eastern area (section one) and was a male approximately 25 years of age. In contrast, a radiograph from a high status burial (number 352) from the eastern area (section three) had a total of one Harris line; it was a male approximately 30 years old (Figure 23).

Conclusions

Radiographic analysis has been used in two widely different archaeological contexts in order to solve specific archaeological problems. This laboratory method in the cases specified has resulted in the discovery of archaeological evidence where hypothesis previously existed. X-ray analysis of ancient Peruvian pottery produced visual traces of the fabrication process, and helped validate Donnan's (1965) reconstruction of Moche ceramic technology. Radiographic analysis also revealed certain other observable characteristics which may be indicative of different and distinguishable ceramic workshops. Further research should result in a much expanded store of evidence which can more fully support or refute such interpretations. Radiographic analysis is shown to be an important tool in the practical reconstruction of ancient ceramic technology, and it is to be hoped that it will enjoy expanded use in future applications.

X-ray analysis was also utilized in order to test an hypothesis by L. King (1969) on the nature of social organization within a skeletal population in Southern California. Because morphological traces of what might be considered social rank (or position) can be detected radiographically, it may be possible to further subdivide King's reconstruction of social stratification at the Medea Creek cemetery. The present evidence suggests that areas of both high and low social status existed in the eastern part of the cemetery, in sections one through three. Section three seems to have been an area reserved for high status burials while sections one and two may have had lower status associations.

Although the conclusions arrived at in both experiments are predicated upon extremely small samples, and should be further tested before being uncritically accepted, both studies underline the practical suitability of X-ray photography for archaological problem solving. While only the areas of ceramic technology and social stratification in skeletal populations have been approached here, it seems clear that many more and different applications of the technique could be made within the archaeological universe.

Acknowledgments

I am grateful to Dr. Chris Donnan, Department of Anthropology, University of California, Los Angeles, for his assistance and guidance in reconstructing Moche ceramic technology. I would also like to thank Dr. John H. Rowe, Department of Anthropology, University of California, Berkeley, and Larry Dawson of the Lowie Museum, for their comments on interpreting the X-rays and for assistance in the subsequent comparative analysis of Moche and Chimu collections at the Lowie Museum, Berkeley. I am also appreciative of the guidance provided by Dr. James D. Collin, radiologist, University of California, Los Angeles, for his guidance in the detection of arrested growth lines.

The Measurement System

The objective of a good measuring system should be to facilitate the accurate determination of the vertical and horizontal positions of any object, regardless of shape or size, which is discovered *in situ*. It should also make it possible to accurately determine the orientation of specimens more than 3 or 4 centimeters wide especially if they are not equidimensional and thus are likely to be preferentially oriented by stream currents or other such depositional forces. The most economical way to precisely locate an object in this fashion is to use a three-coordinate system of measurements which would indicate the distance from the object to known, fixed reference points along three mutually perpendicular axes. In the case of an excavation the logical axes are north-south, east-west, and vertical. Ideally, the primary reference point for each axis should be the same for all specimens since this increases accuracy and makes the measurements easier to translate later. In large excavations however, accuracy and ease of measuring may be increased by establishing secondary reference points at carefully measured distances from the primary reference points.

A frequently used primary reference point for the vertical coordinate is the surface of the ground. Although this is convenient, it is seldom the best choice since the ground may be sloping or irregular, making it impossible to determine the depths relative to each other of widely separated specimens. A better primary reference is an imaginary horizontal plane lying somewhat above the surface of the ground. Since it is almost always impractical to suspend an actual, physical representation of this plane above the excavation and measure down from it, the plane should be symbolized by a single marker such as a firmly set stake marked at the proper elevation to represent a single point within the datum plane. When a measurement is to be made of the depth of a specimen below the datum plane, a leveling device of some sort must be used to extend a horizontal line out from the primary reference point over the specimen, and then the vertical distance from the line to the specimen must be measured with a tape or meter stick.

For the two horizontal coordinates the best primary reference points are already surveyed baselines running due north and east. For large excavations it is desirable to establish a set of secondary reference points by laying out a grid of squares, using the baselines as two lines of the grid. If one set of lines is numbered and the other lettered like a map grid then the position of any square and its contents can be approximately indicated by naming the lines by which the square is bounded. The horizontal position of any specimen within the square can be more precisely determined by measuring the specimen's distance away from the north and west (or south and east) boundaries of the square.

An example of a set of measurements similar to those described above is diagrammed in Figure I. In the case of a small object such as a mouse bone, a small tooth, or a plant fragment, only one measurement needs to be taken along each coordinate, from the center of the specimen perpendicularly to each of the three reference lines. For any object which is small enough that the probable error in measurements may equal or exceed the length of the specimen, to measure the location of more than one point on the object is a waste of time.

For larger specimens, especially those which are oblong or flattened and thus likely to be preferentially oriented by stream currents, more than one point may need to be measured since measuring the location of only one point on the specimen does nothing to indicate its orientation. If the larger specimen is something

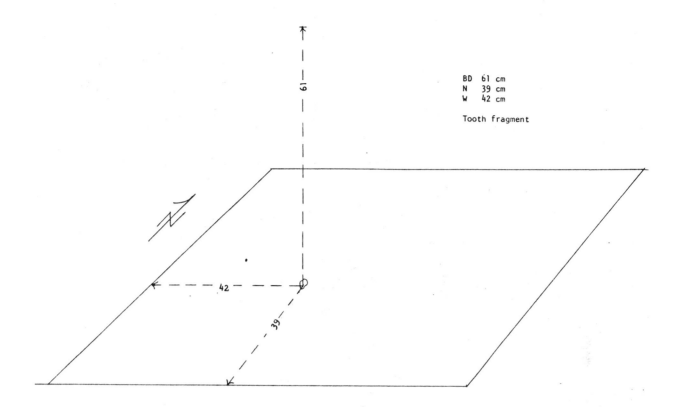

Figure 1: View of a meter-wide grid square showing north, south and below datum measurements for a typical small specimen, with solid lines representing unit boundaries. The broken lines denote the axes along which measurements are taken; figures along these axes are distances in centimeters from the specimen to each reference point.

such as a femur which is oblong with a single well-defined long axis, a system such as that diagrammed in Figure 2 would be highly effective. Three specific points on the specimen are selected and the position of each of these points is measured along each of the three coordinates, yielding nine measurements in all. Two of the points (proximal and distal in Figure 2) always should be at the extreme ends of the specimen's long axis; these define the orientation and position of that axis. The third point should be some easily identifiable feature on the specimen which is as far away as possible from the long axis (in Figure 2, the fovea capita in the head of the femur); the position of this point relative to the other two indicates how the specimen is rotated around the long axis.

This three-measurement system is equally effective for flattened specimens such as scapulae which may not have a single-well defined long axis. For such specimens the three points selected should form the widest possible triangle across the specimen's major plane; in the case of a scapula, for instance, one point might be the center of the articular surface and the other two the opposite sides of the top edge of the blade.

Although best suited to the sorts of specimens described above, the three-measurement system can also be used for more or less equidimensional specimens

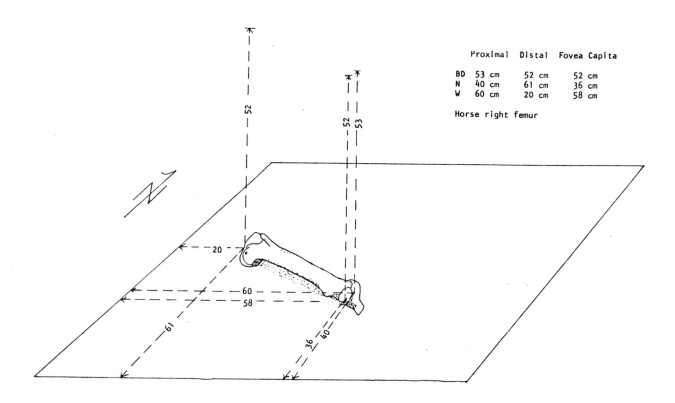

Figure 2: View of a meter-wide grid square showing north, south, and below datum measurements for a specimen of a size and shape which makes it necessary to determine orientation as well as position. Note that three measurements are taken from each point on the specimen to each reference line; these indicate the positions of three different points on the fossil.

as long as they are not so featureless that it is impossible to find three properly spaced and clearly differentiable measuring points. Certainly, if one wishes to definitely establish the orientation of an equidimensional object the three-measurement system is best; however, in most cases it is questionable whether the time needed to make so many measurements on a single specimen is justified in view of the fact that equidimensional specimens do not seem to be preferentially oriented by currents. If the orientation of a specimen is not considered important, or the specimen lacks identifiable measuring points, but is too large to be dealt with by the one-measurement system, a time-saving alternative may be to simply measure the distance along each coordinate of those points on the specimen which are closest to and farthest from each of the three reference lines, indicating, where possible, on which side of the specimen each measurement was taken (Figure 3, for example). Although such a two-measurement system indicates orientation at best only in general terms, it does locate large specimens with somewhat greater precision than does the one-measurement system.

Measuring Equipment and Techniques

Besides accuracy, the principle objectives in choosing measuring techniques should be to measure as quickly and easily as possible, while making the tech-

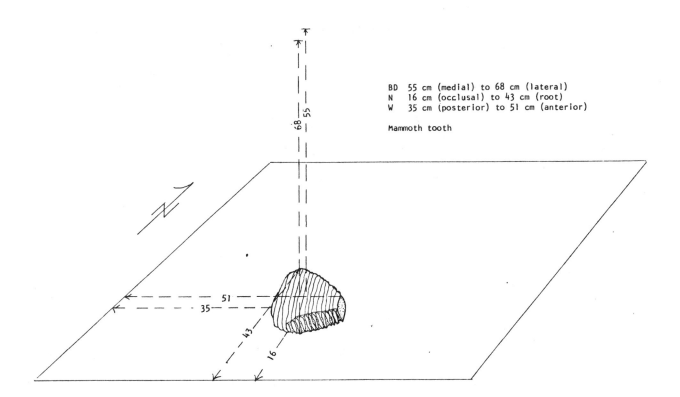

BD 55 cm (medial) to 68 cm (lateral)
N   16 cm (occlusal) to 43 cm (root)
W   35 cm (posterior) to 51 cm (anterior)

Mammoth tooth

Figure 3: View of a meter-wide grid square showing north, south, and below datum measurements for a more or less equidimensional specimen. Measurements along each axis do not necessarily fall at only three points on the specimen, as they did in Fig 2.

niques as difficult as possible to use incorrectly or carelessly. This becomes increasingly important in large fossil deposits because having to take the same repetitive set of measurements on hundreds of specimens each day quickly becomes tedious enough that even the most conscientious worker may become careless, thus introducing unwanted errors into the data. To combat this problem, equipment needs to be made as foolproof and easy to use as possible, something which is fairly easy to do for horizontal measurements but difficult to do for the vertical measurement.

For the two horizontal measurements the best error reduction measure is a carefully laid out grid system in which the lines are no more than a meter apart. This makes it possible to take all measurements with a meter stick (easier to use with accuracy than a flexible tape), and brings the measuring boundary close enough to assure that the stick is held perpendicular to it. It is essential that a transit and steel tape be used to lay out the lines to ensure an accurate north and east alignment of the baselines and that all secondary lines be exactly parallel and correctly spaced. Even with a transit there is likely to be an error of about two centimeters across a grid ten meters wide, but without the transit the error would be much greater. The north and east baselines should be positioned so that their ends can be tied in to permanent landmarks or, if this is not possible, permanent markers should be set up to facilitate later reconstruction. Only the ends of all lines need to be marked, with nails driven into the tops of firmly set stakes, to mark the exact intersections of the grid lines. The boundaries of any

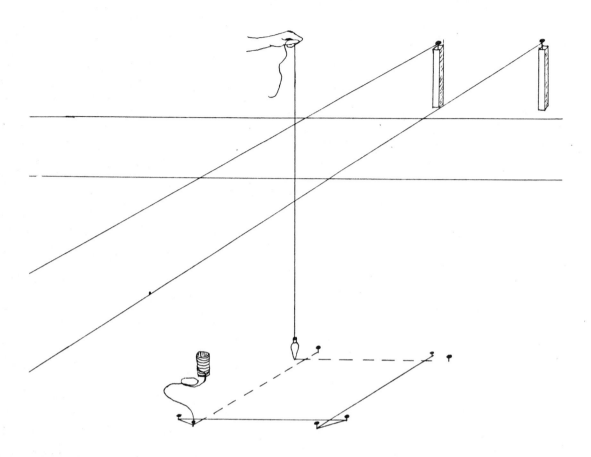

Figure 4: One method of outlining square boundaries on the ground. Broken lines denote the sides of the square which have not yet been marked with string. Note that points marked by the plumb bob for the insertion of nails are beyond the actual corners; this allows for "corner double staking" and eliminates displacement of stakes by digging within the square.

square to be excavated can be marked on the work surface by tightly stretching a chalkline between the nail heads which mark the two ends of each boundary line of that square, and then transferring the position of the square's boundaries to the excavation floor with a plumb bob (Figure 4). The corners of the square can be marked with double headed nails driven into the ground and the boundaries of the square outlined with string. The horizontal position of any specimen within the square can then be measured by holding a meter stick perpendicular to the north or south boundary with its zero point even with the boundary. The other end should extend horizontally over the specimen, making it possible to read off the distances of the points to be measured from that boundary. The process can then be repeated with the meter stick held on the east or west boundary of the square. If care is exercised in the placing of the meter stick, no additional errors should be added to the data by this procedure.

It is more difficult to reduce chances of error in the vertical Below Datum measurements, principally because the plane from which one measures cannot be made as tangible as the boundaries of a meter-wide square; therefore it is hard to be as certain concerning the accuracy of the measurements. The chances of

Figure 5: View of an excavator measuring the depth below datum of a specimen with a line level (the meter stick is being held backwards so that the relationship between its markings and the levelled line will be clear in the photograph). Note the position of the level at the center of the length of cord. At distances of up to 2 meters from the reference stake a level in this central position is fairly easy to read, but beyond this distance problems begin to develop.

error can be slightly reduced by setting up a series of secondary reference points at intervals across the excavation. As with the horizontal baselines, the primary reference point for the datum plane should be a permanent marker, such as a nail in a tree trunk or a pipe set in concrete with an elevation mark cut into it with a file, but secondary reference points may be firmly set stakes to which the datum elevation has been transferred with a transit. As excavation progresses these secondary reference points should be lowered by carefully measured one-meter increments to keep them within a meter of the floor so that a meter stick rather than a tape can be used to make measurements from them. If all measurements involved in setting and lowering reference points are made with a transit, no more than a centimeter of error should be introduced into the measurements by this process, and the amount of error which is avoided is probably far greater.

Unfortunately, this leaves the greatest source of error still to be dealt with: the leveling device used to extend a line out from the reference point to the specimen. The leveling device most widely used by excavators is the carpenter's line level, a small level bubble in a special carrier which can be suspended from a chalk line or other thin cord. One end of this cord is attached to the datum reference point. To measure the depth below the datum plane of a specimen, the worker tightly stretches the cord above the specimen (Figure 5) with the level in the center of the length of cord between attachment point and specimen. The cord is then made level by moving its free end up or down until the bubble in the level centers, and the distance of the specimen below the cord can be measured with a meter stick. This sort of line level measurement is easy to make, and is fairly accurate as long as it is done with great care. However, even minor carelessness can cause serious errors because the line from which the level is suspended has a tendency to sag no matter how tightly it is stretched. At the tensions to which a cord can be stretched by hand, the sag is great enough to make it imperative that the level be placed exactly in the center of the length of cord between attachment point and specimen. This point is difficult to judge by eye, especially since it usually is different for each successive measurement. This problem can be avoided by taking particular care in placing the level correctly each time, but maintaining such a level of watchfulness over a long series of measurements is difficult.

One substitute for the line level, which was developed at Rancho La Brea by the authors with the assistance and advice of other project personnel, seems to eliminate many of the opportunities for error inherent in the line level. This device is similar in principle to the line level, but substitutes a rigid bar made of steel electrical conduit for the flexible cord (Figure 6). In its commonly available length of just over three meters this tubing does not sag enough to necessitate keeping the level in the center of the span. This has made it possible to mount the level on a carriage which can be moved along the bar to a point directly above the specimen, where the level is easy to read. This carriage also has a slot for the meter stick which fits it snugly enough to ensure that it will be held vertical. The fixed end of the bar is mounted on a bracket which can be nailed, screwed, or clamped to a reference stake, with the bottom of the bar at the elevation of the reference point. The attachment between bar and bracket can be made in one of two ways. If it is important to be able to dismount the bar quickly, a hole, large enough to be dropped over a peg on the mounting bracket made of a small bolt, can be drilled in one end of the bar (see inset, Figure 9). This sort of attachment makes the bar easy to dismount. However, when measurements are being taken close to the bracket end of the bar, care must be taken to prevent the greater weight of the free end from causing the fixed end to lift up off the bracket, so spoiling the measurement. The hinge and swivel connection illustrated in Figure 7 is effective in preventing this but makes the use of tools necessary to dismount the bar.

The bracket to which the bar level's fixed end is attached must be positioned on the reference stake from which the measurements will be taken, so that the bottom surface of the bar is at the elevation of the datum plane, or at a carefully measured number of meters below datum. Measurement of the depth of a specimen below datum is made by moving the free end of the bar to a position over the bone or artifact, leveling the bar by moving its free end up or down until the level

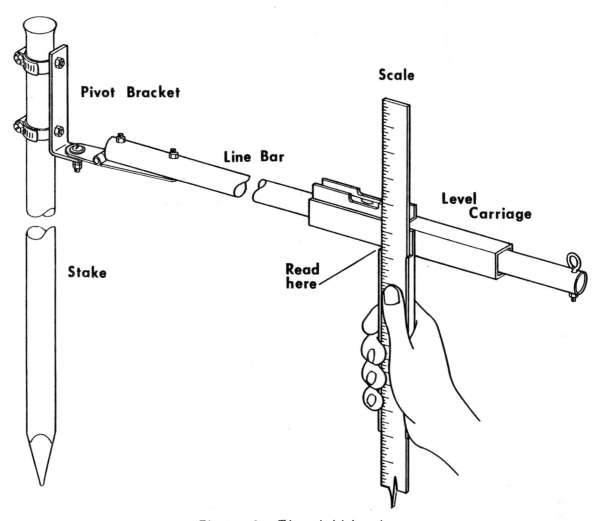

Figure 6:   The rigid level.

bubble centers, and then slipping a meter stick into the slot in the carriage with its lower end resting lightly on the point whose position is to be measured. The depth below datum then can be read from the yardstick against a reference mark on the carriage.

Conclusion

Although the techniques and measuring systems discussed in this paper are the easiest and most accurate to use of those which we know to be practical for making large numbers of measurements under field conditions, they will inevitably allow a certain amount of error to accumulate in the data. If all conditions are perfect, the equipment is carefully maintained and frequently checked for accuracy, and workers are careful and precise, the probable error in measurements across an excavation about ten meters wide might conceivably be as low as two centimeters; for most practical purposes an error this small is of no importance.

The problem, of course, is that conditions are rarely perfect. Besides the factors mentioned above, accuracy can be affected (almost always for the worse)

Figure 7: An excavator measuring the depth below datum of the same specimen depicted in Figure 5, but this time with a rigid level. Note the more convenient placement of the level over the point to be measured.

by many other factors which are different for each excavation site, and sometimes for each day. A general idea of the probable range of error in a site's measurement data can be obtained by selecting at least ten specimens, all of which are exposed in the excavation at the same time, and determining the position of each specimen twice; once with the regularly employed measuring tools and techniques, and then again with a plane table plot, all points of which are shot from a single station. The difference between the two sets of measurements will be somewhere near the minimum error which may be expected in the data as a whole. It should be remembered that opportunities for error vary enough that the results of such a test may be different on successive days; but at least it will provide an idea of whether the data gathered is likely to be sufficiently accurate for the uses to which it will be put, and will help to warn of areas of low accuracy.

Instructions for Bar Level Construction

MATERIALS: Except for the bar, aluminum parts are the most desirable because they are very light and resistant to corrosion; steel, however, may be substituted if necessary. All parts called for can be made from stock hardware; if some sizes of channel are not available, they can be improvised by bending sheet stock into the desired shapes. All construction work can be easily done with hand tools and hand power tools; total cost of materials at 1978 prices is about ten dollars.

PARTS FOR THE LEVEL CARRIAGE (Figure 8)

1: YARDSTICK GUIDE. To be made of channel stock, 8 inches long, $1\frac{1}{4}$ or $1\frac{1}{2}$ inches wide (depending upon the width of the meter stick to be used), with $\frac{1}{2}$ inch flanges. Make a reading point notch at the upper end by cutting down the flanges to what will be the level of the lower surface of the bar after the level has been assembled; the location of this point may be determined by adding the thickness of the top of channel no. 2 to the outside diameter of the tubing used for the bar.

2: CHANNEL FOR BAR. Made of square steel or aluminum tubing, 8 inches long, 1 inch wide. The inside width of this part must be great enough to accommodate the bar (Figure 9, no. 1) but should not be so wide that the bar can be moved from side to side within it; if it is markedly larger a filler (no. 3) will have to be used. If square tubing is unavailable, a substitute can be made from two 1 inch channels having $\frac{1}{2}$ inch flanges fastened together with flat strips (see inset, Figure 8).

3: FILLER. Not needed unless outside diameter of bar is less than inside width of channel no. 2. Make this of aluminum, plastic, masonite, or fine-grained hardwood, of whatever thickness is needed to make it impossible to move the bar from side to side within channel no. 2, but not thick enough to prevent the channel from sliding easily along the bar.

4: GUARD FOR LEVEL. Made of channel, 4 inches long, 5/8 inch to 1 inch wide, with 1/3 to 3/4 inch flanges. Cut out each flange roughly at the center of its length so as to allow the level bubble to be visible from the side.

5: LEVEL. Made by cutting the suspension hooks from a bricklayer's (or carpenter's) line level.

PARTS FOR THE BAR AND PIVOT BRACKET (Figure 9)

1: BAR. $\frac{1}{2}$ inch steel, thin-walled electrical conduit is preferable; 3/4 inch aluminum tubing can also be used but is more likely to bend if tripped over. The steel conduit is available in ten-foot lengths but may be cut shorter; it will probably be useful to provide bars of several different lengths. After cutting, check the tube for straightness by sighting along it or holding it against a stretched chalk line or straightedge. The tubing may be straightened by supporting both ends of the tube and carefully applying manual pressure along its length.

2: EYEBOLT. May be of any convenient size.

3: PIVOT HINGE. Cut off and round one end of a 4 to 6 inch strap hinge, leaving its length approximately equal to its greatest width. Drill a $\frac{1}{2}$ inch hole in the

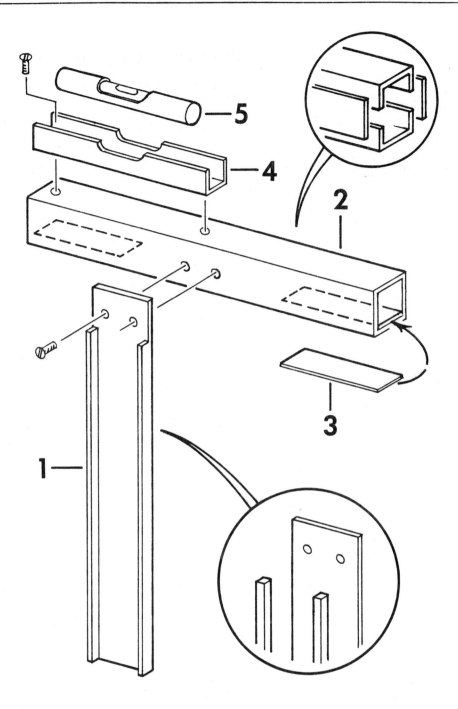

Figure 8: Diagram of the level carriage: insets show alternate methods of fabricating parts which may not be available in the forms called for.

center of that end for the pivot bolt. Note: if a peg mount is used instead of the hinge and swivel, this part is not needed.

4: MOUNTING BRACKET. Made from a 1 x 4 x 4 inch angle bracket. Cut off one end to about 1½ inches and drill a ¼ inch hole in the center of that end for the pivot bolt, or, if a peg mount is desired (Figure 9, lower left) instead of the

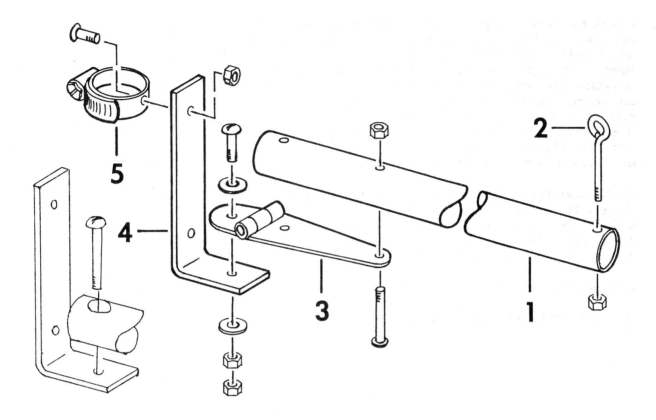

Figure 9: Diagram of the bar and bracket. The peg-type mounting for the bar is shown to the left; this is easier and faster to dismount but is more likely to contribute to errors in the use of the level.

hinge and swivel, drill and tap a hole for a no. 10-24 machine screw or bolt. Drill two holes in the other end of the bracket for the attachment of part no. 5 (a conventional radiator hose clamp) or for nailing or screwing the bracket to a wooden stake.

Assembling the Level

1: Locate and match the attaching screw holes between channels no. 1 and no. 2 so that the two pieces are exactly perpendicular to each other. The pieces should be assembled with no. 6-32 flush-head machine screws (or other screws of suitable size), countersinking the heads and cutting off the ends.

2: If filler No. 3 is needed, attach it to the inside of channel no. 2 with epoxy cement.

3: Center level no. 5 in channel no. 4 and attach with a generous amount of epoxy cement.

4: Drill attaching screw holes ½ inch from each end of channel no. 5 and match and tap holes into channel no. 2. Assemble the level with no. 4, 5 or 6 roundhead machine screws and cut the ends of the screws off flush inside channel no. 2.

5: Check the accuracy of the level bubble (this check should be repeated periodically once the level is in use to make sure that it has not been knocked out of
alignment). To do so, place the carriage unit on the bar, which must be firmly
fixed in an approximately horizontal position. Note the position of the bubble
in relation to the reference lines on the glass. Then remove the carriage without moving the bar, turn it 180°, and put it back on the bar. The bubble should
rest in the same relative position as the first time. If it does not do so, loosen
it and insert thin shims between the channels, under the attachment screw at the
end of the level if it is too low, then re-tighten the screws and repeat the test
until no difference in the bubble's position can be perceived.

6: Locate and match the holes for attachment of bar no. 1 to hinge no. 3; connect
these with 3/16 inch bolts and nuts. Or, if a peg mount is preferred, drill a
single hole in the bar about twice the diameter of the head of the bolt or screw
which will serve as the peg. Drill a hole in the opposite end of the bar for
eyebolt no. 2, so that this hole lines up with the other two holes.

7: The carriage and bar may be painted as long as the level glass is masked first.

8: Place the level carriage on the bar and attach eyebolt no. 2.

THE ARCHAEOLOGICAL FIELD VEHICLE

Brian D. Dillon

Introduction

Discussing motor vehicles as they apply to archaeological field research seems rather prosaic in comparison with the more traditional topics of data recovery methods, laboratory analysis, or new discoveries; perhaps this is why no in-depth treatment of the subject has been published previously. Many archaeologists might even question the need for such a review, for on the surface there seems no more need to study the archaeological field vehicle than the mason's trowel with which we presume all archaeologists are equally familiar. Is there any reason for an archaeologist to be concerned with the kind of vehicle to select, how to drive it, and how to keep it running? Should this be part of his or her practical education? Should the archaeologist spend any time becoming familiar with the characteristics of particular makes and models, or any money modifying them mechanically? Are the demands made upon vehicles called into archaeological service any different from those of the anthropologist, botanist, or geologist? Does an "ideal" or a "universal" archaeological field vehicle exist?

Chairborne archaeologists will spend little time considering such questions, for field research problems and their solutions occupy them seldom if at all. Field archaeologists, on the other hand, have a basic concern with vehicular efficiency because they understand that research projects succeed or fail as a direct result of the logistical aptitude of the project leader and his crew. By professional mandate, the field archaeologist must get to his site, get the investigative job done, and then move the field notes, collections, film, equipment and personnel out with a minimum of damage to all. Mundane logistical matters must be mastered before the labor and time available to the project can be devoted to archaeological problem-solving, or the venture will never get off the ground. Experienced field archaeologists recognize logistical self-sufficiency as their most primary criteria for success; in the realm of transportation, this means that once the project begins, it should not be halted or slowed by vehicular problems and that such problems should be remedied by the archaeological group itself. The alternative to vehicular self-sufficiency is, of course, to make the project dependent upon an outside individual or organization that has no vested interest in its success and no reason not to delay it or to unnecessarily deplete its financial resources.

Unless the field researcher is independently wealthy, is willing to devote a lifetime working at sites in his own home town or within the reach of public transportation, logistical reason argues for the careful selection and intelligent use of archaeological field vehicles. Constraints of geography (or access) and economy will certainly dictate choices in this realm, at least in part. Choosing the wrong vehicle can limit the number or the type of sites accessible to the archaeologist and his crew; if transportation breaks down halfway to the project location, less productive (but easily accessible) sites may have to be investigated instead. Conversely, many large areas remain archaeologically unexplored because researchers mistakenly believe them to be inaccessible. Familiarity with the proper kind of field vehicle might prove the actual situation otherwise and allow the archaeologist to open up such regions to scientific enquiry. By the same token, if the researcher depends upon the wrong kind of vehicle for an exploration project, yet is oblivious to its limitations, his or her results will be incomplete, for such limitations have the habit of dictating geographical coverage.

Generally speaking, the most valuable archaeological sites for investigation are desirable precisely because they are inaccessible, or thought to be. Lack of easy access usually guarantees that post-abandonment disturbance in the form of vandalism or looting has been minimal; therefore the first archaeologist on the scene often has a nearly pristine deposit to work with. The field archaeologist who boasts that he has never investigated a site he couldn't drive onto in his family sedan, then, has surely blinded himself to the existence of what may be the most productive sites in his study region.

Economic considerations involve the investment of time as well as funds, and the wrong field vehicle can hamstring a project through unnecessary transportation delays just as easily as it can bankrupt it through unexpected expense. Driving the wrong vehicle may use up three weeks of research time in reaching the project location, whereas driving a suitable one may take only a week on the road; the difference of two weeks' field research time is either gained or lost in this instance in a used car lot or while reading the want ads instead of while behind the wheel. When the archaeologist spends more time attending to ailing vehicles during a field project than he does to archaeology, the same wrong decision has helped to limit his research effectiveness and may end up ruining his project. The wrong vehicle can require constant repair and need daily attention if it was not designed or modified for travel over terrain characteristic of the project location, and many an archaeologist has found to his or her horror that more than half of the fieldwork budget (which could have been used either to prolong or to intensify the project) has been spent on vehicle rental, repair, or on a fuel bill greatly in excess of what it might have been had a different vehicle been chosen.

If a vehicle is selected that is too small to adequately transport the project crew and its equipment, a second vehicle may have to be rented or purchased, necessitating a 100% increase in monetary outlay. The mechanically naive archaeologist who decides that the only vehicle fitting his field requirements is the one costing $15,000.00 new may also be unpleasantly surprised when his grant proposal or contract bid is rejected because the transportation budget is too high.

The same archaeologist will be chagrined to see a competing project purchase and modify four used vehicles for the same $15,000.00 and obtain four times the mobility, logistical independence, or time effectiveness that he could have had.

Field vehicles play stellar roles in many an anecdote told around archaeological camp fires, and most researchers with more than a year of experience in the field abroad or in desert or tropical rain forest environments can usually cite instances in which a dependable vehicle "saved" the field project from disaster. Unfortunately, many more stories feature vehicular villains: perhaps the conveyance broke down constantly, or it used up every available dollar, or it had to be abandoned and the project was forced to terminate early.

Like many field archaeologists, I have spent hundreds of hours working on both good and bad field vehicles, patching them back together with wire and pot metal fragments found by the side of the road. I have also reconnoitered many a meleagrous salvage emporium in search of spare parts, or made the wrong part fit like " a true knight of the junkyard," as one leading archaeologist so aptly describes the common persona. Because of this, I am still surprised at how certain vehicular oversights occur again and again in archaeological field situations, and the general level of vehicular ignorance manifested by most archaeology students. This is not to say that I have not committed my share of vehicular *faux pas*, for I have. Indeed, I know of no other archaeologist who has ever had the engine of his borrowed vehicle break loose from its mountings and come to rest in the road only one kilometer over an international boundary. Although a parts outlet was within easy reach in the country I had just left, the vehicle was registered on my passport and I could not use the outlet because customs and immigration requirements forced me to improvise with what was locally available (in this case, nothing) within my new host country.

In a different country, I saw a visitor to a field project I was working on break an axle on the first day of his trip; his car must have been the only make and model of its type in the entire hemisphere, and needless to say it was towed off the road and remained under a shed roof for the remainder of the field season. In yet a third country, an associate stranded with the wrong kind of vehicle during the rainy season in a remote area saw fit to do some road improvement work using as ballast the masonry from thousand-year-old temple pyramids, while in a fourth country another associate, unfamiliar with her vehicle and with her own capabilities, managed to park her four-wheel drive once in the Pacific ocean just before high tide and once in quicksand over a kilometer up a creek from the nearest firm ground. It is therefore not surprising that a few archaeological research institutions do not trust their scientific staff with the task of driving but instead supply professional chauffers to get the field researchers to and from their sites.

Most field projects cannot afford such luxuries, however, nor can their participants commute on a daily basis from their domiciles to the field location; fewer projects still can be reached through public transportation. Like it or not, most archaeological field endeavors depend very heavily upon motor vehicles for the basic requirements of personnel and equipment transportation, supply of essentials, and for emergency escape. No matter how efficient any given transportation system appears to be or how well suited a particular vehicle is to the project requirements, some saving of purchase or of upkeep cost can usually be obtained through a greater familiarity with what has surely become one of the researcher's most helpful logistical tools: his archaeological field vehicle.

Selecting a Field Vehicle

Because many archaeologists spend a good deal of time inside vehicles en route to project locations, most such individuals are familiar with the shortcomings and the advantages of their particular make and model. Unfortunately, this knowledge usually comes at a time when it is impossible to modify the vehicle in order to increase its efficiency or to exchange it for something more appropriate to the needs of the specific project. The best transportation may in fact not be a conventional motor vehicle at all, but a motorcycle, a boat, a mule or a dogsled, depending upon local topography and availability.

Motor vehicles may be completely out of the question because of excessive cost, the unavailability of fuel, licensing or permit problems, the probability of theft, or other reasons, and some different means of terrestrial transport must be found for personnel and supplies. In such circumstances, mules or mule-drawn carts may be the best solution (Banks and Dillon, this volume). In some extreme situations, even animal power is impracticable because mules or horses cannot be rented, sufficient food cannot be found for them, disease or rustlers or some other problem prevents the archaeologist from making use of them. In such cases, only two options remain: either abandoning the project or relying upon human motive power. In the tropical rain forest, any passageway must be constantly defended against encroaching vegetation, and this can either be done mechanically (with a bulldozer) or manually with machetes. The best vehicle for use here may in fact be a small bulldozer, but only if the archaeologist's ecological conscience permits it. A "swamp buggy" with oversize flotation tires (large enough to float the vehicle across streams and swamps) is another option, but roads must be kept clear for this machine as well. A specially rigged bicycle familiar to many as standard in Southeast Asia or a four-wheeled cart may in fact be the only wheeled vehicle practical for a rain forest project (Fig. 1), and these usually will have to be built by the archaeologist himself. In desert areas, a balloon-tired wheelbarrow may be the ultimate choice, whereas in arctic climes the archaeologist may find himself relying upon a snowmobile or dogsled.

While each different vehicle type or make and model presents certain advantages for a specific application and disadvantages for others, most archaeological projects are fairly standard in their requirements: the most common functions that the field vehicle is called upon to perform include transporting personnel, transporting equipment, providing a safe storage place, and providing an ambulatory workshop and tool chest. This being so, is not a single kind of vehicle, such as the family car, best suited to the many conflicting demands arising from archaeological application? Not really, because the two most basic demands upon the field vehicle (the ability to travel over rough terrain and the ability to carry a large load a long distance) historically have led automotive designers to produce radically distinct vehicles. Vehicles made to transport a large number of people comfortably over long distances with all of their gear are not necessarily suitable for fording streams or scaling volcanic slagheaps once the destination has been reached. By the same token, the vehicle that can negotiate very rough terrain often has very expensive fuel consumption habits and costs too much to drive to the field project location and back again. The best vehicles for the situation outlined would therefore be, first, a large station wagon with small engine, and second, a four-wheel drive jeep-type vehicle. Since it is usually impractical to tow one behind the other until a specific need is felt, a better solution would be to find a single vehicle that is a compromise between the two extremes; this would probably be a truck with a very good range of gears and a powerful engine.

Figure 1: *The archaeological field vehicle in its most basic form.
Above: Two-wheeled, hand drawn cart with pneumatic tires.
Salinas de los Nueve Cerros, Alta Verapaz, Guatemala, 1975.
Below: Four-wheeled, hand drawn cart with iron wheels, loaded
with outboard motor, 17 gallons of fuel, tools, supplies and field
equipment. Salinas de los Nueve Cerros, 1978.*

In selecting an archaeological field vehicle, budgetary considerations should include weighing the original purchase price against the eventual upkeep expenses; both estimates must be made with a firm knowledge of the kinds of demands that will be placed on the vehicle in the field. A very inexpensive used truck with many power accessories and automatic transmission, for example, may cost twice as much to run as the same vehicle with standard transmission and is therefore not economical in the long run. By the same token, a four-wheel drive vehicle that climbs the steepest hill imaginable but which costs $10,000.00 is not necessary or even desirable if it is constantly in the shop having transfer case components serviced or if the same hill can be conquered by five different used vehicles costing $2,000.00 each by simply driving around it.

There are many vehicular types and models available to the archaeologist: sedans, station wagons, light trucks, heavy trucks, vans, jeeps, 4 x 4 trucks, 6 x 6 trucks, and so forth, and almost as many engine types. Many vehicles can be ordered either with gas or diesel power, sometimes even with propane, and the same engine will have radically different output depending upon whether or not it has been equipped with smog control devices. Conversely, a six-cylinder engine need not be more powerful than a four-cylinder, nor need a V-8 engine consume more gasoline per mile than a four or a six. Selection of a field vehicle may have less to do with the specific array of makes and models available than with a firm knowledge of basic vehicular types and how they function; in fact, of the thousands of makes and models that have appeared over the past few decades, most are now extinct (Georgano, 1968). Archaeological requirements, because they involve moving fairly large crews, delicate field equipment, and heavy artifact loads over long distances and rough terrain, are different from those placed upon the vehicle by the businessman, the botanist, and even the geologist or ethnologist. Functional considerations, therefore, should guide the selection of a vehicle rather than loyalty to any particular make or model, and the one chosen must be the most practical for the specific or general situation in which it will be used.

Automobiles made during the early decades of this century were much more akin to trucks and tractors than to what we recognize today as the family car. This is because the roads of that period were little better than dirt tracks; hard pavement was rare and few banked curves existed. As most archaeological projects require considerable travel over surfaces identical to those for which the cars of the teens and twenties were designed (Figure 2), perhaps a brief look at some of the basic characteristics of a typical automobile of that period is in order.

The Model T Ford enjoyed production for almost twenty years (1908 to 1927) essentially unchanged; over fifteen million were made because it was perfectly suited to the roads and to the economic situation of its time. It was a success because it was inexpensive to purchase, cheap to run, easy to repair, simple to find parts for, easy to modify, and, most importantly, it could go almost anywhere. The Model T was geared low, had very good road clearance, and few inessential features or concessions to comfort or vanity that added weight, reduced power, or unnecessarily complicated its mechanical operation. It could carry either a fairly large payload, or six passengers, through mud, sand, or slush without mishap.

The family car of the present day, by contrast, has between one-half and one-quarter of the Model T's ground clearance, weighs at least a ton more than it did, and usually features a very large engine that gets low gas mileage because

Figure 2: Normal archaeological road conditions. Two-foot deep ruts in a stretch of the Guatemala-Honduras spur of the Panamerican Highway, 1974.

it is burdened with accessories such as power steering, power brakes, air conditioning, an automatic transmission, and complicated smog-control devices. Besides diminishing the power delivered to the driving wheels (which is, after all, the primary function of the engine), such features add a great deal of unnecessary weight, reduce the engine's life expectancy, and often are composed of modular or "plug-in" components that cannot be adjusted or fixed but must be discarded and replaced by brand new units when something goes wrong. In many cases the car will only run on one kind of gasoline (such as unleaded) and cannot even be tuned by its driver because it has fuel injection instead of a carburetor, and electronic ignition instead of a distributor and breaker points. Not only will body styles change each year, but often engines will be redesigned with increases or decreases in displacement which ensure that pistons, cylinder heads and other parts are non-compatible between model years. Since 1958, this has been the general trend in the United States with but few exceptions, and it continues today even though most manufacturers are producing smaller and less powerful vehicles. The post-1958 family car, then, is fine for travel over paved surfaces and for trips no farther than a day's journey from the nearest dealership or auto parts store but in most cases is completely unsuitable for archaeological field use.

What kind of vehicle is best for use on field projects? There are two basic kinds, which can be categorized as either special or general purpose. A highly specialized vehicle, such as a small jeep or a five-ton dump truck with hydraulic lift, is often appropriate for a long-running project where the vehicle can be stored during the off seasons when not in use. Such a vehicle need only be driven or shipped once to the project location and will more than justify the additional expense upon arrival if the need exists for it. Most archaeological projects have less specialized needs, however, and general purpose (or compromise) vehicles can be expected to serve in a variety of different contexts continuously over a long period of time. In fact, the general purpose vehicle must serve as several different special purpose vehicles equally well, and in many different locations. The rule of thumb in selection should be that a special purpose vehicle should be bought only if no other vehicle can perform its function at least 50% of the time. This is because in nine cases out of even the worst ten, for example, four-wheel drive is unnecessary and the experienced driver can go just about anywhere with two-wheel drive. The one situation where four-wheel drive may be required can usually be overcome by the two-wheel drive vehicle and its driver by use of a winch, shovel, length of carpet or by a minimal amount of road work before driving over the area in question, or by simply backing up and trying a different track or road. By the same token, a five-ton dump truck becomes unnecessary if the driver of a half-ton pickup is willing to make ten trips to the backdirt pile instead of one.

The general purpose vehicle is a compromise between different specific functions which may be mutually exclusive in terms of design dictates. The specific requirements of the field project in question and the archaeologist's familiarity with road conditions and terrain at the project location will be the most crucial factors in selecting such a vehicle. The archaeologist who must drive only 100 miles from the home institution to get to his or her project location but who, upon arrival, must constantly cope with traveling through fine sand, deep mud, or unstable shale should probably opt for a four-wheel drive truck or jeep-type vehicle. In this case, the poor fuel economy of such vehicles is more than compensated for by the efficiency of the vehicle over surface conditions that would defeat most two-wheel drive vehicles, but only because the location is so close to the point of origin. If getting to the project location, however, involves driving several thousand miles over good to poor roads (Fig. 2) and four-wheel drive is never absolutely essential at any time at the project location, a two-wheel drive vehicle becomes the only logical choice. A difference in fuel consumption of between 6 and 20 miles per gallon may not be too important within the context of a project in the next county or state, or when the vehicle will only be used occasionally; but when a 10,000 mile round trip must be made in order to do archaeology, such a difference can easily bankrupt the project or force its abandonment.

The vehicle selected should be a relatively common make at the project location (not necessarily at the place of purchase), so that parts stores or at least dealerships will be familiar with it. There should be plenty of identical or nearly identical models still running at the project location so that local mechanics will have some familiarity with its idiosyncracies and so that local wrecking yards can be expected to have at least a few of the same model for cannibalization when spare parts are required. The model should also have been in production long enough for its strengths and weaknesses to have become common knowledge; these can be learned from other owners/drivers of the same make, and individual vehicular life-histories can be compared. The vehicle should neither be so old that spare parts have gone out of stock or are obsolete, nor should it be so new that spares have not reached out-of-the-way dealerships or parts outlets. Vehicles meeting all of these requirements will, of course, vary in different parts of the world. Ford or Chevrolet pickup trucks, for example, would seem best suited for use in North and Central America, Land Rovers for most of Africa, older Volkswagen buses for western Europe, and Toyota Land Cruisers for most of Asia. A rotary-engined truck would be a poor choice for use in a country exclusively populated by piston-driven vehicles, as would a 1962 Borgward station wagon be for use in Alaska or a 1954 Studebaker truck in Costa Rica.

The vehicle selected must be as simple to run and to work on as possible, and should have a high degree of parts interchangeability with other makes and models. It should not be so delicate that jerry-rigging broken parts or forming replacements out of similar parts but from different engines will cause its premature demise. Therefore, the best choice of vehicle would be the most recent model in a long-running line, or an early model in the same line that has been recently rebuilt. Such a vehicle would have a chassis and body style basically similar for many years, and should accept a variety of different engines, transmissions, and running gear. It is a very good idea, before purchase, to investigate how many different engines of different displacements, cylinders, and the like will fit the transmission that comes with the vehicle, and vice versa, as well as on how many such engines a supposedly "interchangeable" part such as a water pump or distributor, will fit.

The three most important qualities of an archaeological field vehicle are durability, dependability, and economy. In engine size, bigger is not always better. For example, in one common make of truck, a single model can accept either a 327 or a 350 cubic inch block. The 350 gives only a slight increase in power over the 327, yet introduces many more problems. Because it is simply a 327 block bored over, the 350 has less internal strength, poorer cooling properties, and is more prone to blow head gaskets; its fuel consumption in some cases can be up to 25 percent more. By the same token, a four-cylinder engine may not be substantially more economical than a small V-8, for it has higher rpms than the V-8 at almost any given speed, and will wear out much faster than the larger engine if neglected. A four-cylinder engine usually will have a productive life span of only 100,000 miles or so before a rebuild is necessary; some require valve grindings every 10,000 or 25,000 miles for continued running efficiency. Most American-made V-8 engines can be expected to run (with proper maintenance) for up to 150,000, and in some cases for 200,000, miles before rebuilding, and this may cancel out any four-cylinder advantages in economy through fuel consumption. Even a three-quarter-ton truck with a small V-8, two-barrel carburetor, four-speed or overdrive transmission, and radial tires can get around 20 miles to the gallon if the cruising speed is kept low and the driving is consistent, while many four-cylinder vehicles in off-road contexts or on poor roads will not average much more than 22 or 24 miles to the gallon.

The field vehicle should have a high power-to-weight ratio; this is found more easily in a lightweight vehicle than in an over-powered engine. The vehicle should also have good road clearance so that rough roads, streams, sand, and mud patches can be negotiated without breaking the undercarriage, oil pan, or differential and so that the vehicle does not get high-centered. Ground clearance is not the same as body clearance, for a jacked-up body is not proof against getting stuck because this only increases the clearance between the body and the tires. Tall tires on large wheels are the only way to achieve substantial ground clearance, and a vehicle should be selected that offers at least six to eight inches between the lowest point on the body frame, or running gear (usually the differential) and the ground. If this degree of clearance is not present, either the vehicle will have to be modified or another vehicle chosen.

The general duty vehicle should have a transmission geared for low rpms at top speed in high gear in the interest of fuel economy and at the same time should have a lowest gear (usually a compound or "granny" low) that can approximate the traction offered by a four-wheel drive system. It should be large enough to carry the entire project crew and all of their equipment, unless the project is so large that more than one vehicle is required. It should also be secure enough for the safe storage of all valuable field equipment and camp funds. Under no circumstances should the archaeological field vehicle have an automatic transmission, power brakes, or power steering, for these options add quite a bit of expense to the purchase price, increase fuel consumption up to 25 percent, and diminish problem solving capabilities to an extent not acceptable in a field vehicle. A vehicle cannot be gravity-started with an automatic transmission if the battery goes dead, and often a vehicle abandoned for a short time while the driver is in search of a battery recharger is found beyond salvage upon his return because of the attentions of vandals or parts thieves. Nine times out of ten, a drained battery can be recharged by the vehicle's own charging system if that vehicle can only be started; this is, of course, an impossibility with an automatic transmission. With an automatic it is difficult to brake using the engine on mountain roads, or when heavily loaded, and this tends to put undue wear on the brakes and tires. Most power steering and power brake systems function only when the engine is running. If the engine stalls, as frequently happens under field conditions of adverse terrain, poor or impure fuel, and so forth, the driver can find himself unable to steer the car or to stop it when and where he desires until he can get the engine started again. These shortcomings are not usually a problem in the driveway at home, but in the field can mean the difference between vehicular destruction and serious injury or merely a bothersome delay.

The archaeologist selecting a field vehicle, even when funds are plentiful, must decide between new and used transportation. Many new trucks cost in the neighborhood of $8,000, and most four-wheel drives begin around $10,000. A used vehicle in very good mechanical condition will almost always cost as little as one-half the price of a new one and can provide savings of up to one-fifth the total purchase price new. Maintenance costs, however, rise proportionately to the age of the vehicle, and the time and expense that will be involved must be considered. Shipping a used one, and the greater frequency of repairs in a faraway location cancels out any financial saving that may have been made over the purchase price of the new vehicle. This is because shipping costs are based upon weight rather than on the vehicle's total value. When considering a new model, however, it is important to recognize that many new "field type" vehicles have features that render them useless in an archaeological field situation. This is because the increasing suburban market for such vehicles has encouraged manufacturers to load them down with appurtenances more reminiscent of the family sedan than of an off-road vehicle. Because such new vehicles are becoming more and more expensive yet less and less suited for hard use under adverse conditions, it often makes very good sense for the archaeologist to purchase a used vehicle.

Any used vehicle has, of course, already had a certain percentage of its total usable life span expended, and in this regard cannot compare with a model just off the assembly line. At the same time, however, many ten- or even fifteen-year-old vehicles were built so well that after an engine rebuild they will have a much longer life-expectancy than a brand new truck or four-wheel drive. The number of 1942-45 Willys Jeeps still running is ample testimony to this, as well as to how little we have come to expect from new vehicles today. Perhaps the best way to adjudge the probable longevity of a potential purchase, or to prognosticate future problem areas, is to visit several wrecking yards and inspect a sampling of vehicles identical to the one being considered for purchase. The archaeologist buying a used vehicle must accept the inevitability of having to make repairs and purchase new parts in much greater frequency than would be the case with a brand new model, but the low original purchase price usually allows for even major repairs to be made without the total financial outlay approaching the cost of a new vehicle. Driver confidence in a used vehicle is increased if the new owner knows exactly what has been replaced or rebuilt; working on the used vehicle will not only result in a more reliable piece of transportation equipment but constitute advanced training that will be essential for problem-solving in the field.

Certain rules of thumb apply to the purchase of used vehicles, and these can always work to the advantage of the buyer. A dented body that looks bad but is still structurally sound, for example, will result in a lower price but should be of no concern to the archaeologist. A vehicle with excellent running gear and body but a blown engine or wrecked transmission can often be bought for only a few hundred dollars; a new engine or transmission will cost no more than a thousand dollars, and a like-new vehicle can often be obtained for a total investment of less than $1500. It is always best to buy a used vehicle that has not been subjected to extensive off-road travel, for there is no way of knowing what abuses it has been exposed to. A heavy-duty vehicle that has been mainly used on the street can often be converted to off-road use much more inexpensively than a beat-up off-road vehicle can be repaired if it has seen hard usage. For example, you can expect to pay no less than $500 to have a frame straightened if your newly-purchased off-road truck or jeep has hit one rock too many. A two-wheel drive vehicle should never be purchased with the idea that it can be converted to four-wheel drive inexpensively. Unless unlimited time, money, and a complete machine shop are available free of charge, this is an impossibility. While purchasing a used vehicle always involves a certain amount of risk, the practical advantages are great, for often a project can buy five used trucks for the price of a single new one, or use the money saved to hire five times as much labor, run forty more carbon dates, or stay in the field for several additional weeks or months.

Driving Habits

As an instructor who has sent more than one student off in the project vehicle on a simple errand only to be told some time later that the truck has gotten mired up to its door sills in an Olympic-sized mudhole, or that a helpful volunteer has managed to flip his jeep onto its roof while climbing a too-steep hill too fast (fig. 3), the need for a brief review of driving habits in the field seems rather obvious to me. Other instructors might feel that such a discussion is not only unnecessary but silly, yet usually change their minds when the new student backs the project truck into a tree and destroys both, or drives the project vehicle into a 2 x 2 meter excavation unit and prematurely forecloses it, or, worst of all, happily and obliviously drives over the accumulated level bags and concomitant artifacts collected during the field season.

The most basic rule to be followed is that practice makes perfect, and unless the field director intends to do all the driving, he or she should provide members of the field crew with the chance of solving driving problems and making minor repairs through local practice before the 10,000 mile round-trip begins. All crew members who are going to drive the vehicle should be trained before the trip and should be tried out under the most adverse conditions. Find the worst possible road in the immediate vicinity of the home institution, and have the individual students or drivers practice on it until their confidence level will let them tackle the worst that the project location has to offer. A few good mudholes and sandtraps should be located, and each project member should be given the opportunity to drive through them and

Figure 3: Common hazards. Two views of vehicular disaster at LAn-218, The Corbin Tank Archaeological Site. Above: Four-wheel drive vehicle after flipping over onto its roof. Below: Two-wheel drive vehicle sunk over its axles in a deep mud hole. Los Angeles, 1981.

get the vehicle unstuck if it becomes bogged down. The advantages of having your crew learn how to do this where a tow-truck is only a phone call away over waiting for the real thing should be self-evident. If the neophyte finds that he can not drive out of the hole he has driven into and has to pay a towing bill, the same mistake will probably not be repeated some time later on a wind-swept steppe or a sun-blasted desert. Negotiating steep hills, rutted roads, and shallow stream crossings should all be part of the archaeology student's training. Prior familiarity with the vehicle and with the kinds of terrain to be traversed will provide the neophyte field driver with enough confidence in his ability to master a real problem situation so that it should never occur to him to panic. Panic is dangerous because it leads to the conviction that disaster is the inevitable outcome of any problem situation. A heavy vehicle stuck in soft sand at the base of steep cliffs that is going to be under water once the tide comes in will be lost if its driver panics, for example. The calm driver, on the other hand, will simply get out and release air from the tires until they have enough traction to pull the vehicle out, and then will drive out of danger. The difference between the two options, obviously, lies in the fact that the successful driver has already practiced the crucial activity that can save the vehicle.

One of the best reviews of off-road driving habits is provided by Waar (1975:13-36), I recommend this to those new to the problems of driving heavy vehicles in difficult terrain. In general terms, the two most common problems encountered while driving around out-of-the-way archaeological sites are (1) a lack of traction, and (2) excessive grades. A lack of traction on a paved surface is usually caused by excessive water, snow or ice; most city drivers are used to coping with this problem. A lack of traction off pavement is caused by the road surface being too soft to bear the weight of the vehicle. The universal result, regardless of whether the road surface is composed of sand, dust, mud, snow, or gravel, is that the vehicle gets stuck. Once stuck, nothing that can be done inside the vehicle will get it unstuck. Road work, jacking, or tire-deflation are the only means of getting out of the problem. Soft surfaces can be negotiated successfully if the vehicle is kept rolling steadily in low gear without any rapid changes in acceleration or in braking; these will make the tires cut through any hard crust that may exist and trap the wheels in the softer material that lies below.

The best way to avoid getting stuck is to "read" the terrain before driving over a problem area. Usually this involves nothing more complicated than getting out and walking for a few hundred meters to test the ground surface. It is much easier to get a leg unstuck that has dipped into mud over the kneecap than it is to pull out a three-ton vehicle mired up to its bumpers. In desert areas, dry lakebeds often look firm and hard and seem to provide welcome relief from the jarring of constant travel over a rocky "desert pavement." Such surfaces, however, are often silty or sandy and will trap a heavy vehicle, and it is a better idea to select a gravelly or stony passage. The same rule applies to fording streams; only a sleepwalker will drive into a stream without knowing the depth of the water in it, and, more importantly, the condition of the stream bottom. Six inches of water over a silty or muddy bottom is much more dangerous than two feet over a hard gravel surface, but the distinction cannot usually be made without getting out of the vehicle and wading with a depth-stick before driving across. If the stream cannot be forded at the first location, there are two options: either drive the vehicle to a different location where fording is possible, or modify the water level or streambed. The latter can often be accomplished by building a small dam so as to lower the water level at the ford, or by laying an underwater path of stones to be driven over, or by anchoring planks underwater so that the vehicle does not become mired. In some cases, bridges will have to be built. It should be obvious that it is much less work to back up and find another ford location, even if a delay of a day or two is involved.

At the other end of the spectrum, in extremely dry, brushy areas, one should always find a clearing in which to park before stopping. A dry creosote bush or tall grass jammed against the header pipe or exhaust manifold can easily come alight and torch the gas line, and the entire vehicle can be lost.

Other common road hazards are snags or rocks in the road which can puncture tires or damage running gear (and even occasionally flip the vehicle over), and steep hills. Stalling a heavy vehicle halfway up a very steep hill is an unpleasant experience, especially when the trail is covered with loose sand or gravel and assorted large rocks and tree-stumps. In this situation, attempting to turn the vehicle around so that it can be "nosed down" the hill usually results in flipping it over on its side, and therefore it must be backed down under constant braking in its own tire ruts. This is difficult to do without assistance. The easiest method is to have all the passengers get out and help guide the driver back a bit at a time.

Some hills that seem insurmountable can actually be climbed by putting the vehicle in reverse gear; this will work if reverse gear is lower than the lowest forward gear, or if the carburetor float valve cuts off earlier with the vehicle facing uphill than facing down. Few hills that look like they can be negotiated are actually too steep to drive up; what defeats the vehicle is the combination of extreme slope and lack of traction. Once gravity begins to work against the forward power of the engine and any momentum that was built up during the approach, a stall or a slide is often the result. Here, as with the unfordable stream, the only option is to back up and try another way around.

An important part of driver training that is often neglected deals with automotive terminology. This becomes crucial when the archaeologist is piloting a vehicle in a foreign country for the first time. Besides being able to convert English distance and volumetric measurements to the metric system so as to avoid being over-charged for fuel or ticketed for speeding (see Table 1 for conversions), the driver should be familiar with the nomenclature for parts and tools in the language of the country he is driving through. Fortunately, most non-Western languages use loan words from English, French or German for most automotive parts, but if the driver is not conversant with, for example, Spanish yet desires to drive to the Darien, some additional preparation should be made. Mechanical dictionaries do exist in most European languages (cf.: Saiz, 1968); failing this, the archaeologist can compile his own checklist of commonly used terms.

Table 1:
Metric to English Conversions.

Kilometers to Miles		Liters to Gallons	
1	.621	1	.264
2	1.242	2	.528
3	1.864	3	.792
4	2.485	4	1.056
5	3.107	5	1.320
10	6.214	10	2.640
15	9.321	15	3.960
20	12.428	20	5.280
25	15.535	25	6.600
30	18.642	30	7.920
40	24.856	40	10.560
50	31.070	50	13.200
60	37.284	60	15.840
70	43.498	70	18.480
80	49.712	80	21.120
90	55.926	90	23.760
100	62.140	100	26.400

Maintenance

Any vehicle, if not maintained, can rapidly be converted to an expensive pile of junk. Maintenance is a bother, but nothing is as important in protecting the financial investment made in a field vehicle as changing its oil regularly, and checking the air, water, and brake fluid levels. The two basic items of maintenance equipment are literary, rather than mechanical, and consist of the vehicle's bench or owner's manual and the driver's maintenance record. Most newer vehicles (1963-1983) have very detailed manuals available, either from the manufacturer or from an "aftermarket" publisher. Two such manuals covering a good span of model years would thus be Chilton's (1980) *Repair and Tune-Up Guide: Ford Pickups, 1965-1980*, and Clymer's (1980) *Chevy & GMC Pickups, 1967-1980: Shop Manual*. For older vehicles, encyclopedia type reference volumes covering many different makes may be the only listings available with tune-up data, wiring diagrams, etc.; Chilton's (1971) *Auto Repair Manual, 1954-1963* is one of the better offerings of this type. Such manuals provide the manufacturer's specifications for the vehicle in question, and usually have very useful keys to troubleshooting or diagnostic information that can be used to detect problems before they become major. These manuals should be used in conjunction with a maintenance record for the vehicle that keeps track of when and what kind of service was supplied. In any situation in which more than one individual will be driving the vehicle, such a service record is essential. It also has the happy facility of keeping track of who paid for gas, oil, etc., on what day with what funds, and greatly simplifies accounting for grants or for reimbursements. An example of such records is shown in Figure 4. Needless to say, both the maintenance record sheets and the shop manual should be kept in the vehicle at all times.

If at all possible, only one person should be responsible for maintaining the field vehicle; this eliminates the possibilities for confusion which occur when a series of different drivers all presume that someone else has been putting the necessary oil in the engine. Service should be at regular intervals as specified in the owner's manual, but if the vehicle is more than ten years old, service should be done at least 1/3 more frequently than suggested. On very prolonged trips or those over very rough country, problems that would be minor under casual use can develop into fatal ailments very rapidly, so it is a very good idea to check the vehicle every 24 hours or 500 miles, whichever comes first.

The oil filter should be changed at least annually; where excessive running in low gear or operation with inferior oils is unavoidable, it should be changed every 2000 to 4000 miles. Aftermarket options for converting a single oil filter to a dual system do not excuse the vehicle from this schedule of changing filters. Oil changes every few thousand miles will prolong an older engine's life almost indefinitely, and special additives can help as well. STP and various Bardahl products actually increase the lubrication properties of oil, but it should be remembered that oil has a very specific function (to lubricate) that it should be recognized that some additives (such as detergents) actually impair this function. If the oil has not been changed for some time, or if the engine is old, or if poor-quality oil has been used, the oil change should be preceded by flushing the motor out with a clearing agent. The engine should not be run longer than a few minute with the "motor flush" in it, for this can severely damage it. Flushing breaks down sludge and varnish, and clears clogged oil passages; this produces a cleaner engine to introduce the new oil to. Cranking the engine with the coil lead disconnected, and oil plug and oil filter out will completely drain dirty oil from the system, and make the oil change more complete.

Two basically different types of oil are on the market: non-detergent single viscosity oil, and multi-viscosity detergent oil. Multi-vis oil is supposed to thin out at cold temperatures (so as to aid starting) and to thicken up at hot temperatures so as to properly lubricate engines in areas with great seasonal extremes of temperature. The detergent which is added is supposed to aid in keeping oil journals and lines free of sludge, and to break down varnish. Single weight oils, on the other hand, do not change consistency greatly as a result of air temperature, but will go

DAILY VEHICLE LOG

Project:_____   Date:_____

Starting Point:_____

Beginning Mileage:_____ (Recorded by):_____

Drivers: _____ (From _____ AM/PM to _____ AM/PM)

_____ (From _____ AM/PM to _____ AM/PM)

_____ (From _____ AM/PM to _____ AM/PM)

_____ (From _____ AM/PM to _____ AM/PM)

Fuel: _____ (liters__/gallons__) @ _____ total cost, paid by _____(Receipt)

_____ (liters__/gallons__) @ _____ total cost, paid by _____(Receipt)

_____ (liters__/gallons__) @ _____ total cost, paid by _____(Receipt)

Oil: _____ (liters__/quarts__) @ _____ total cost, paid by _____(Receipt)

Other parts or supplies (include cost and receipt #:_____

_____

_____

Maintenance: Oil Level_____ Checked by:_____ @ _____(AM/PM)

Water Level ___ Checked by:_____ @ _____(AM/PM)

Tires _____ Checked by:_____ @ _____(AM/PM)

Lights, Horn, Mirrors, Wipers, Gauges, etc._____

Potential problems noted for correction:_____

_____

Ending Point:_____

Ending Mileage:_____ (Recorded by):_____

Total day's mileage:_____ Total day's expense:_____ Total road hours:__

Figure 4: Maintenance record in the form of a "Daily Vehicle Log". Copies of this should be kept in a binder and filled out in any field situation where there is more than one driver per vehicle, or on long trips. Besides keeping track of upkeep activities, the form organizes the record of financial outlay, which simplifies accounting after the project's conclusion.

"thicker" or "thinner" depending on the operating temperature of the engine. The standard single weight for the temperate zones is SAE 30; constant running at very hot temperatures (or for use in worn engines) would require 40 weight oil, while running in very cold climates would require SAE 20 weight oil.

Field vehicles running under strain should not use multi-viscosity oils. Because these oils contain detergent, they actually have less pure oil per quart than single weight non-detergent oils do, and they wear out faster and lubricate less. Detergents are only needed if the vehicle's owner never changes the oil, or does not use motor flush periodically. If the vehicle is left sitting for a period of months or years, the acids that can form from detergent multi-vis oils will eat through soft metal bearings and prematurely shorten the life of the engine. Enough cans of oil for at least one change should always be carried in the vehicle; this is not so much for use during an "emergency" oil change as when the oil pan is accidently punctured, and you need something to refill it with after it has been repaired.

In some countries gasoline is of such poor quality that unless special precautions are taken, continued running will severely limit the efficiency of the vehicle. This is especially true in places where underground storage tanks are not cleaned regularly and much sediment, rust, scale, and grit accidentally becomes admixed with the gasoline or diesel fuel. In some areas, profiteers "water" the gasoline for increased profit, with frustrating results to the unsuspecting archaeological driver. In-line gasoline filters can eliminate much of the danger to the carburetor and engine occasioned by impurities in the fuel, and several spares should be kept for regular replacement. Some filters are made with a removable element that can be cleaned out and re-used; the best of either type will have clear glass or plastic casings so that you can determine visually whether or not fuel is reaching your carburetor if your engine stalls. Fuel filters should be mounted just before the carburetor or the fuel pump (or in both places); sand or grit passing through the fuel pump can ruin it, so a dual-filter system may be more economical than keeping a spare fuel pump on hand.

Some vehicles feature cooling systems that are "closed" or sealed, and are therefore not ever supposed to require maintenance. This is a myth, and vehicles operating under hard usage or in desert areas should have their radiators inspected frequently and water or coolant added as necessary. Water should only be added to a hot engine while it is idling; this ensures that the thermostat is open and that water is circulating through the system and that the level seen in the radiator is the actual level throughout the entire cooling system. The cooling system should be flushed at least once a year, and for normal operation no more than ½ the total fluid volume should be a commercial coolant. Radiators that spring leaks can often be repaired simply by pouring a commercial brand of "stop-leak" compound into them, but it should be remembered that this is only a temporary measure that can have deleterious results in other components of the cooling system. It is always best to mechanically repair any leak in the cooling system rather than trusting to a chemical "patch" that can dissolve at the worst possible moment or detach itself and circulate through the system and jam either the water pump or the thermostat. At least a gallon of pure water should be carried in the vehicle for emergency use, and under no circumstances should radiator water ever be used for drinking, cooking, etc., even in the direst emergency. Freeze plugs often become corroded and spring leaks, especially in older engines. These can often be temporarily patched by cutting a rubber plug from an inner tube the diameter of the freeze plug's interior, and then by screwing the patch over the plug with a sheet-metal screw; stop-leak in the system will complete the patch from the inside.

Air filters are often neglected, and an extremely dirty one can cut the engine's "breathing" down remarkably. If the vehicle can be started, a dirty filter can cut fuel efficiency down to 75% of what it should be; this is because the carburetor, set to mix approximately 14 parts air to 1 part fuel, is having its air supply reduced to 12, 11 or even 10 parts, and the engine is burning excessively rich. If the air filter is of the "throw-away" element type, several spares should be on hand. Oil-bath filters are the best option in extremely dusty or sandy areas; these have fallen out of favor recently because they are so messy, but they are extremely reliable. If a new replacement filter cannot be found for the cartridge type, the old element can sometimes be re-used after it has been banged and blown clean with compressed air. Other custom filters are made of foam rubber encased in wire mesh; these elements can be removed, soaked in kerosene or gasoline, and re-used.

When a vehicle runs poorly because of a clogged filter, it is tempting to run it with the air intake on the carburetor unguarded. This should be avoided, for all it takes to ruin an engine for good is running it for ten seconds through a sand storm or ten minutes through heavy blowing dust, and no driver can predict when such will occur. An emergency filter can be made by punching holes in the old, clogged one, and then covering the new apertures with mesh or cheesecloth. When replacing an element, always bring the old filter into the parts store so as to effect a visual match; do not trust the numbers in the catalog, or the blandishments of the salesman who has never been under the hood of your project's vehicle.

Periodic checks of the battery should be made, especially if you are driving under a load, or in very hot weather. The electrolite level should be visually inspected every few weeks, and distilled (or at least boiled and strained) water should be added as needed. An inexpensive, pocket-sized hydrometer can predict when a battery is going bad, and is a wise investment. Maintenance-free batteries have become increasingly popular in recent years, but can cost up to 50% more than the old type. Other electrical system maintenance includes rotating fuses in their sockets every year or so, to keep them from becoming cemented in place, and cleaning dirty or oxidized terminals or connections.

Archaeological field vehicles tend to have very poor tire lifespans. This is not usually due to excessive wear as much as it is to traumatic injury and punctures. Tire rotation can extend the overall lifespan of a set of four tires under normal operating conditions, but is not of much use in off-pavement driving because the rear tires will often wear out much sooner than the steering tires in front (unless there is a major alignment problem). Also, when the front and rear tires are different in size or in tread pattern, it is a mistake to rotate them.

Two different kinds of tires are suitable for the field vehicle; radials or high-traction non-radials. Radial tires are stiffer, generally have a fairly small tread pattern, and take higher inflation pressures than normal bias or belt-ply tires. Radials have great advantages over conventional tires for long-distance travel because they provide less resistance to the ground or pavement and more "roll," which results in lowered gas consumption. Because they have less "give" than regular tires, however, they are not particularly well-suited to to off-pavement travel, and in fact tend to bog down more frequently than bias-ply tires with knobby treads. Radials do tend to have a much longer tread life than bias-ply tires , and are not really more expensive than the more radical "high-traction" off-road bias-ply offerings. High traction tires, because of their knobby tread pattern, are able to "grip" unstable or loose surfaces better than radials, but since less rubber is on the ground within any given tread area, they tend to wear out rapidly. High-traction tires are wasted if used for normal transit on paved surfaces; thus, the ideal field vehicle might have two complete sets of four tires which can be changed as the need arises. This solution is, of course, economically unfeasible for most projects, and the usual compromise is to have high-traction tires on the driving wheels and radials on the steering wheels, the two mounted spares will then be of the type most suitable to the demands of the project, and will contribute to the creation of a complete set of either radials or high-traction tires. It is illegal in some areas to mix radials and bias-ply tires on the same vehicle for pavement use, but such restrictions do not usually apply to off-road travel.

On long trips or while driving over tortuous terrain, tire pressure should be checked daily. Either a sliding pocket gauge or a dial gauge should be used, not the standard "big-toe" method. Depending upon the load, the average speed of driving, and whether the tires are bias or radial ply, are tubeless or have tubes inflation pressures may vary between the front and rear pairs. Pressure should be identical, however, within each pair. Tire pressure should be taken only after running the vehicle some distance so as to allow the tire and the air inside to heat up; tire pressure "hot" will always be greater than tire pressure "cold" despite the fact that no air has been added. Running at high speed for extended periods of time tends to make tire pressures increase, especially if tubes have been introduced to normally "tubeless" tires. A tire that was running at 50 psi on day one through the low desert may cool down overnight so that it only reads 35 psi on the morning of day two; filling it to 50 psi while cold and then running over a ground surface that heats up to 120°F will drive the internal pressure up to a point at which a blowout may occur, so periodic checks are necessary if much driving is done between radically different climatic zones. The effects of altitude can also possibly influence blowouts; filling tires to the maximum at sea level in Veracruz, for example, can lead to disastrous problems three or four hours later when one drives over the pass of Cortez into the Basin of Mexico at around 9000 feet elevation. Any good owner's manual will specify inflation pressures appropriate for the vehicle and kind of tire in use; these will also have charts showing how to recognize abnormal wear patterns.

Spares and Repairs

Auto mechanics engage in the practical application of the scientific method every day, by attempting to prove individual components within a system defective until they are known to function correctly, and then by doing the same with entire systems until all problems have been isolated and solutions can be applied. The archaeologist, because of his or her training in systematics and basic interest in technology, should have little trouble thinking like a competent mechanic when a vehicular problem arises, but in fact many archaeologists proclaim mechanical helplessness. A good rule for the field archaeologist to follow is "if you drive it or ride in it, you should be able to fix it." Any archaeologist who plans to explore or excavate in central Africa, tropical South America, or eastern Alaska must be able to anticipate situations in which, for example, the vehicle stops with three flat tires, a punctured radiator, blown head gasket, dead battery and too much water in the gas tank simultaneously. Mental preparation for such events is provided by a number of texts (Sclar 1976).

The field vehicle must get the archaeologist to the project location as well as serve for weeks, months, or years as transport for personnel and equipment, as a prime mover for towing or pushing other vehicles or objects, and as an ambulatory workshop, tool shed, and safety deposit box. In light of these demands, the least the archaeologist can do is to keep the vehicle running. Preventive maintenance and immediate corrections of problems are singularly important. It is a truism that when the vehicle stops dead in its tracks, it is a rainy, moonless night, and the nearest mechanic is several hundred miles away but the closest thief or vandal is just around the corner. Vehicles never seem to break down on nice dry, level surfaces, but most frequently in axle-deep mud; the day or night is either so cold that metal tools stick to your hand, or so hot that the afflicted part of the vehicle cannot be touched without burning your fingers. Being able to fix a broken truck when everything is going right therefore becomes somewhat of a minor achievement for the archaeologist; the real acid test is being able to fix it when everything is going wrong.

The only way to make certain that this goal can be accomplished is for the archaeologist to be absolutely self-sufficient in the following areas: (1) in mechanical knowledge and experience in problem-solving specific to the vehicle in question; (2) in having the necessary owner's and/or bench manual and specifications for correct tuning and repair of the vehicle; (3) in having a tool kit adequate for all diagnostic functions and also equal to the demands of most repair jobs; and (4) in having a basic selection of spares for those parts most likely to need replacement under heavy and protracted use, or those which can immobilize the vehicle if broken, lost or stolen.

The most basic rule in vehicular repair is to stop and investigate the minute you suspect something is malfunctioning. The archaeologist in a foreign country with his or her vehicle registered on his passport cannot afford to ignore the warning signals of his conveyance, for in most cases one cannot leave the country without the vehicle. The driver and all passengers must learn the audible "vocabulary" of normal and abnormal noises so that problems can be identified. Alert driving involves all the senses; an unfamiliar smell may be the harbinger of wiring about to burst into flame, a new vibration could presage one of the front wheels losing its lugnuts, and a whining sound may indicate a water pump about to freeze up. The point is that if even one cannot immediately repair a broken or breaking item, he or she should be able to diagnose the problem so that the trouble is not compounded through ignorance. If it is too dark, windy, or cold to effect repairs, it is best to wait until daybreak or a lull in the storm. If you have to leave the vehicle to get a part welded, or to visit a repair shop, be certain that someone stays with the vehicle to protect it from vandals and parts-strippers. If this cannot be done, hire a local person to keep an eye on it and promise him or her a bonus if everything is untouched upon your return.

Figure 5 lists the most important tools, spare parts, and compounds that are necessary for corrective surgery on vehicles in isolated or foreign contexts. It should be noted that some of the major spares (such as the water pump, etc.) need not be new; in fact, violating the first rule of mechanics ("if it works, don't fix it") have have some advantages in this situation. Installing a new water pump and keeping the old one as a spare results in the knowledge that both work, instead of the common situation in which the brand new spare is found to be incorrect many miles or months after it has been purchased. Most repairs in the field take the form of disassembly and re-fabrication rather than direct replacement, and the archaeologist should have some familiarity with this process. Common sense is required in most regards; for example, since most unitary chassis parts exist in bilaterally symmetrical pairs, the patterns for a damaged wishbone, spring shackle, etc., can usually be obtained from the surviving unit on the other side of the vehicle. Any time an unfamiliar unit or system is disassembled, diagrams should be drawn of the sequence and positional relationship of all parts so that they can be put back together in the correct way. When replacing parts at a junkyard or store, always try to carry in the broken part so that a correct match can be obtained. If modifications are necessary, such as tapping new holes, or grinding projections off, this should be done before the part is brought back to the vehicle. If the original part cannot

Figure 5: Checklist for tools, spare parts and supplies that should be carried in the archaeological field vehicle during extended trips or in rough areas.

DIAGNOSTIC TOOLS

1: Shop Manual
2: Timing Light
3: Tach/Dwell Meter
4: Compression Tester
5: Tire Pressure Gauge
6: Hydrometer
7: Circuit Tester
8: Feeler Gauges
9: Spark Plug Gauge

CORRECTIVE TOOLS

10: Combination Wrench Set
11: 10 or 12" Crescent Wrench
12: 6" Crescent Wrench
13: Torque Wrench
14: Socket Wrench Set (3/8 or 1/2)
15: Socket Extensions
16: Socket U-joint
17: Socket Wrench Step down/up
18: Breaker Bar for S.W.
19: Spark Plug Socket for S.W.
20: Impact Wrench Drive
21: Hex Wrench Set
22: Oil Filter Wrench
23: Adjustable Pliers
24: Vise-Grip Pliers
25: Needle-Nose Pliers
26: Wire/Sheet Metal Cutter
27: Large (12") Phillips Screwdriver
28: Large (12") Slot Screwdriver
29: Small to Medium Slot Screwdrivers
30: Small to Medium Phillips "   "
31: Metal Chisel
32: Metal Punch
33: Ball-Peen Hammer
34: Putty Knife
35: Flat, Round, Triangular Files
36: Sand Paper
37: Easy-Out (Extracter) Set
38: Metal Drills/Drill
39: Gear Puller
40: Valve Spring Depresser
41: Hacksaw
42: Siphon Tube/Brake Bleed Tube
43: Oil Filler Spout
44: White Paint (Liquid Paper)

EMERGENCY TOOLS

45: Flashlight
46: Flares
47: Fire Extinguishers
48: Lug (X-bar) Wrench
49: Hydraulic Jack
50: Sheepherder's Jack
51: Tire Pump

52: Crowbar
53: Wheel Chocks/Jack Blocks
54: Shovel
55: Bucket
56: Rip Saw
57: Machete
58: Axe
59: Length of Carpet
60: Towing Chain
61: Towing Rope

SPARE PARTS

62: All Hoses
63: All Belts
64: All Gaskets
65: All Fuses
66: All Filters (x 2 or more)
67: 2 Sets Spark Plugs
68: 2 Sets Points, Rotor, condenser
69: Distributor Cap
70: Plug Wires
71: 2 Mounted Tires
72: 2 Inner Tubes
73: Water Pump
74: Oil Pump
75: Gas Pump
76: Carb Rebuilt Kit
77: Timing Chain
78: U-joints

EXPENDABLE SUPPLIES

79: Oil (enough for change)
80: Rear-end/Trans. Oil
81: Wheel Bearing Grease
82: Engine Oil Flush
83: WD-40 or Liquid Wrench Spray
84: 3-in-1 Oil
85: Carburetor Cleaner Spray
86: Quick-Start Spray
87: 1 Quart Brake Fluid
88: Radiator Flush
89: Radiator Stop-Leak
90: Gasket Paper
91: Gasket Sealer
92: Heavy Duty (Ignititon) Wire
93: Light Duty (Accessories) Wire
94: Assorted Electrical Connectors (clip, spade, bolt-on, etc.)
95: Electrician's Tape
96: Tube Patch Kit
97: Assorted nuts, bolts, screws, washers, cotter pins, etc.
98: Epoxy or Super Glue
99: Duct Tape
100: Hand Cleaner/Rags

be detached from the vehicle, a careful drawing of it should be made (with accurate measurements), for correct identification at the source of supply; a series of polaroid photographs here will save many headaches and needless extra trips.

Tools are generally either analytical or corrective, and can be further divided into general or special purpose. A valve-spring depresser designed for your particular engine is a special-purpose corrective tool because it performs only one corrective function; a tach/dwell meter is a general purpose analytical tool because it can perfrom several different analytical tasks. It is relatively easy to overstock the tool kit, but this is preferable to taking too little. In rural areas in some countries it is conceivable that the well-stocked archaeologist's tool kit is the most complete in the town or even in the province. Because of this, a sturdy tool box with lock is a must. Some people, especially unscrupulous mechanics in rural areas, will stop at nothing to obtain a good set of tools, so these should never be left out overnight or even exposed to public view very much. A special and preferably locking cabinet should be installed in the vehicle carrying the tool box. This will provide additional security while making the tools accessible when something goes wrong.

Bulky or extremely heavy tools should be eschewed. A portable welder, for example, may come in handy once or twice, but the low potential demand for it, coupled with the availability of such units for hire, legislate against either buying or transporting one for the field vehicle. By the same token, the archaeological field vehicle should have other tools that are neither analytical nor corrective in the sense that they can facilitate repair; these are essential for simply getting the vehicle unstuck once it bogs down in deep mud or sand or finds its way blocked by a fallen tree or rockslide. This tool category would include a shovel, bucket (for either draining mud holes or for carrying gravel with which to fill them in), length of carpet (to provide traction in sand or mud), an axe, machete, and saw, at the very least.

The rule of thumb for selecting spare parts is similar to that for tools; spare cylinder heads, for example, are not necessary, but head gaskets certainly are. Spare parts should be packed carefully so that they are not damaged through unnecessary impacts, rusting, and so forth; when an old part is removed, it should be kept for customs purposes and for possible remanufacture if the new spare just installed also goes bad. A list of spares carried in the vehicle should be typed up and kept with the bench manual. This greatly facilitates customs inspections and lets any person who did not actually buy the parts know what is immediately available at hand. This latter bit of planning avoids the common duplication of effort any time more than one driver or mechanic is involved in a repair job. A listing of all tune-up settings and useful information such as plug type, idle speed, and the like, should be typed up and pasted inside the door of the glovebox of the vehicle for ready reference. Point and plug gaps, timing BTDC, and so forth, should be painted in white or flourescent paint on the inside of the hood or on the firewall as well, so that simple corrections can be made without recourse to a manual when one is under the hood in the rainy dark.

Modifications

Very few new or used vehicles are well suited for archaeological use in the field when initially purchased, and the archaeologist usually has to correct mechanical or organizational shortcomings himself to make the vehicle fit the specific requirements of his project or projects. Modifications usually involve deleting superfluous features or systems and adding new parts or systems to increase the safety of the vehicle, to render it more secure from theft or vandalism, or to increase its efficiency. Increasing the efficiency of a vehicle usually involves making changes in the engine and power train to provide for longer life-expectancy, greater fuel economy, and increased dependability. Changes in the chassis, suspension, running gear, and body are made to increase ground clearance and make the vehicle more resistant to the field conditions which most archaeologists must operate under.

Safety

Safety conditions should dictate two distinct kinds of modifications: those made to help avoid accidents, and those made to increase protection if an accident should occur. In this context it is important to think of accidents that can immobilize the vehicle as well as those that might endanger the driver and passengers, for the former are much more common than the latter. The best way to avoid accidents in any vehicle is to be aware of the location and velocity of all other vehicles in the vicinity, to make their drivers aware of your presence, and to be able to spot hazards early enough to avoid them.

In most trucks and many four-wheel drive vehicles, rear vision is extremely limited, and stock mirrors are inadequate for general use in the field. The field vehicle should have both large flat mirrors as well as spot mirrors on outriggers on either side; the flat mirrors should be adjusted to reveal the vehicle sides and the road area immediately behind, while the spot (or slightly fisheye) mirrors should be adjusted to provide for wide lateral vision. Mirrors should be easily adjustable, so that different drivers do not have to strain in order to use them, and should also be detachable so that they can be removed and locked inside the vehicle in areas or countries where they are compelling targets for thieves. If the outriggers (or mirror braces) are prone to vibration, a metal scrap can either be welded or bolted on to stabilize them. Some outriggers come hinged or spring-loaded so that they can be folded back parallel to the vehicle side; this feature allows passage in very narrow tracks and eliminates the danger of instant breakage if the mirror strikes a stationary object. Off-road driving, especially at night, should not be attempted without a proper set of mirrors, for backing up and renegotiating dead-ends is a constant chore, and dangerous if rear vision is limited.

Many trucks and four-wheel drive vehicles cannot stop as rapidly as passenger cars, and thus extra caution and correct lighting are essential for night driving Off-road travel at night in rough areas is especially hazardous if inadequate lights are used, and lack of forward vision after dark is responsible for most off-road accidents in which the vehicle gets stuck, breaks an axle, or overturns on too steep a hill or too deep a ravine. In addition to the standard lights, extra off-road high-beams should be installed that focus in advance of the regular beams. These will light up obstructions at a great distance and allow the driver to avoid them or to choose a new route. Additional high-beam lights can be attached to the top of the cab or to a roll-bar, or suspended from a roof-rack, and should have a separate dashboard control switch. A single fixed high-beam facing backwards will often prove invaluable when backing up at night, and a hand-held spot light can be used to inspect the engine at night, to illuminate road signs that the headlights can't reach, or to focus on the road when a steep hill forces the driver to look out the side window when the hood blocks his view.

If lights and mirrors are essential equipment for avoiding potholes and road hazards, they are no less crucial in warning the driver of the approach of oncoming traffic or pedestrians; to cope with this danger the driver must also have an early warning system in the form of a very loud horn. Most "stock" horns cannot be heard by the driver of another vehicle at any great distance, especially if road noise is excessive or if the radio is playing. As a vehicle (and concomitantly, its horn) gets older, the sound generated by the horn becomes progressively weaker, and many ten-year old horns have only a fraction of their original volume. Instead of a brand-new replacement identical to the original equipment, a single or dual trumpet compressed air horn should be substituted. These are two to three times as loud as standard horns, and generally have a longer life-expectancy; unfortunately, they can cost up to twice as much as a stock replacement horn, and will take more time to install. Air horns are very useful in countries where pedestrians are unused to motor vehicles and tend to endanger themselves by walking, sitting, or sleeping in the roads, and are also good for signalling while on site survey if exploration parties become separated.

When or if an accident occurs, certain modifications previously made to the vehicle will make the difference between the driver and passengers being carried away from the scene or walking away under their own power. If the project location is in extremely rough or mountainous country, a roll bar is good insurance against overturning. Roll bars can be either bolted or welded to the frame, and must be designed for the specific vehicle involved. Unless selection is made with care, the wrong kind of roll bar will severely limit storage or passenger space, or render parts of the body or chassis inaccessible for repair. Roll bars should be padded so that head injuries will not occur to the passengers during a roll-over.

Seat belts should be availabe for all vehicle passengers, and should be bolted through the floor (not to the seat itself) and anchored with wide flat washers. Safety belts should have quick-release catches so that escape can be rapidly made from a burning or overturned vehicle; either safety racing belts or push-button release belts are preferable to the kind that thread through a tension clamp. Shoulder harnesses are not always suitable for off-road travel, especially if forward vision over the hood becomes limited while climbing steep grades

Heavy bumpers and skid plates do more, of course, to protect the vehicle than the driver during a collision, but should still be installed on a field vehicle. Ramming the front end of a stock vehicle into a sharp bedrock outcrop can completely destroy the engine, front suspension, and radiator; chances for damage are considerably lessened if a heavy-duty front bumper and engine/transmission/transfer case skid plate(s) have been substituted. Skid plates should be bolted, not welded to the frame so that they can be easily removed and straightened if they become bent and should be perforated so that oil or fluids can be drained or added as necessary without the removal of the entire skid plate. Vertical front bumper extensions (or cowcatchers) are useful if much driving is done in high brush or if the vehicle is often used to push other vehicles; in the event of a collision with large animals such as deer, cattle, or horses, these can actually save the vehicle from serious damage. Rear bumpers made box-fashion from welded plate stock should be large enough to use as a step, and should have a towing ball either attached directly or a provision made for a detachable towing rod and ball.

Final safety considerations do not involve permanent modifications to the vehicle , but instead relate to common sense equipment in the vehicle. At least two fire extinguishers should be carried, and these should be checked periodically to see if pressure has been maintained within reasonable limits. All drivers and passengers should know how to operate the kind of extinguisher carried, and should actually practice getting it from its storage location and simulating its operation. At least one extinguisher should be within reach of the driver inside the cab, either bolted to the roof, firewall, or floor, and should not be covered by other equipment or delicate items that cannot be removed in a hurry. If the archaeologist is using a truck with camper shell, or if the passenger or cargo compartment is in any way isolated from the cab, then a second fire extinguisher should be easily accessible in the passenger area. A third installed under the hood in the engine compartment provides cheap insurance against gas or electrical fires. Other safety equipment that should be carried includes a complete first-aid kit, which should be under the front seat, and visual warning devices. Visual warnings can be effected through highway flares, portable reflectors, or battery-powered flashers; the cheapest and most highly recommended option is to simply plaster the back, sides and front of the vehicle with reflecting tape so that it is unmistakably recognizable as a stalled vehicle if one is forced to stop at night in an inconvenient spot.

Security

When expensive or irreplaceable field equipment is stored inside the field vehicle, it must be guarded against hit and run break-ins. In most foreign countries, vehicles crossing the national border are entered upon the owner or driver's passport, and that person cannot leave without the vehicle, regardless of whether he sold it, wrecked it, or it was stolen from him; therefore there is an additional incentive to guard against larceny. Archaeological fieldwork often dictates that the vehicle be parked some distance from the project or the field camp location, and thus it cannot be guarded all the time. While this often is not much of a problem, nevertheless in some areas unless precautions have been taken, unattended vehicles might be stripped of all accessible parts, or stolen, or set on fire, or otherwise vandalized in a matter of minutes. Vandalism can often be avoided by removing provocative bumper stickers, decals, or signs from the vehicle. In some countries, vehicles with foreign plates are sometimes selected for vandalization, so a partial solution is to cover the license plate with mud which can be removed at any time for an official inspection. Vandalism accompanying an attempt to burglarize or steal the vehicle can be avoided if the potential thief can be made to believe that it is too much trouble ot break into the vehicle, or that he has no chance of starting it or driving it away. Antitheft precautions, then, take the form of either keeping the thief from stealing the vehicle or from stealing articles from inside the vehicle.

The clearest signal to a thief that a truck or jeep is not worth breaking into is a steering wheel lock, visible through the windshield. This lock has two hooks separated by a telescoping shaft, and is placed between a spoke in the steering wheel and either the clutch or the brake pedal shaft. When in place, the vehicle cannot be steered or driven away, although it can be towed. Any vehicle's engine can be started without the ignition key if a thief can get into the engine compartment and connect an electrical lead from the low-tension lead on the distributor to the battery; to circumvent this, a hood lock must be installed. An internal hood release mounted under the dash is not proof against hotwiring, for the hood can be raised easily after the cab has been broken into, and the best hood lock available is a length of chain connecting a bar that fits into a key-locking slot between the hood and frame.

Other antitheft devices designed to frustrate attempts at starting the engine are a gas line lock or a secret ignition or battery kill switch, hidden somewhere unexpected and kept in the "off position" while the vehicle is parked. If the vehicle has multiple gas tanks, the tank selector switch should be positioned on an empty tank or in its "neutral position", or, if the vehicle has an electric fuel pump, a simple on/off switch should be installed in an inconspicuous place; either will ensure that even if the vehicle can be started by the thief, only the gasoline in the carburetor float bowl will be available for the getaway and the vehicle will run out of gas in a matter of minutes. Gasoline tank filler caps should lock, and if more than one tank is used, make certain that all caps work off a single key.

All valuables should be kept out of sight in locked storage compartments, so that the temptation to break into the vehicle is minimized. In many parts of the world, the best way to store valuables is in a steel strongbox welded to the floorboards or frame and secured with a hardened steel lock. If valuables or irreplaceable equipment are to be stored in a pickup truck with camper shell, the windows in the shell should be covered with either a strong mesh grille or by steel bars or straps on the inside; sliding windows connecting cabs and camper shells should have a hinge grille that can be swung out of the way for quick exits during emergencies but locked in place when the vehicle is parked. Burglar alarms are of little utility in the field, and if the strong suspicion exists that the field vehicle will be stolen or vandalized, the threat can best be met by detailing members of the crew to sleep in the vehicle on a rotational basis. If this practice seems warranted, modifications should be made for the comfort of this guard and for means of defense from inside the vehicle.

Convenience and Comfort

Modifications which increase the comfort of the driver and the convenience of the passengers are important, for these can help keep riders and drivers alert and able to respond quickly to dangerous situations. Such modifications usually are planned so as to eliminate fatigue, or to keep unnecessary distractions to a minimum. If long-distance driving is required, rotating relief drivers at regular intervals will enable the vehicle to be driven as much as 24 hours per day, and will lessen the potential for slow reaction time that can occur when any single driver has been behind the wheel too long. Many rotational schemes can be tried, but the best system, of course, is to have at least one relief driver resting or sleeping comfortably while another is actually piloting the vehicle. The best way to accomplish this is to build a padded sleeping platform that will allow the relief driver to rest comfortably at full length. These can easily be accommodated by pickup trucks with camper shells and by larger four-wheel drive vehicles, but are impractical in vehicles with short wheelbases or open tops. A vehicle thus modified can also serve as sleeping quarters for one or more project members at the field site, if necessary.

Small additions to keep the driver alert are a radio and/or cassette player to eliminate monotony or highway hypnosis, an adjustable fan in hot areas, and pedal extensions and seat pads if prolonged driving produces discomfort or cramps. If glare is a problem, tinting the upper half of the windshield can help solve the problem; painting the hood a flat black can eliminate much of the reflected brightness. If the vehicle is a pickup truck with camper, a sliding rear cab window is a good idea for communication with passengers or for access during inclement weather.

Storage compartments can be built into most vehicles and will provide more economical use of available space than cardboard boxes and tools, spares and equipment can be locked into easily accessible compartments instead of buried under the load being hauled at the moment. Welded steel roof-racks allow heavy or bulky items to be carried out of the storage or passenger area of the vehicle and will create more usable space inside while at the same time rendering the items carried outside more accessible. Objects placed on roof-racks should be lashed in place and, if valuable, secured with locks and chains. Too much weight on a roof-rack can alter the vehicle's center of gravity, so the driver should supervise loading.

When the field vehicle gets stuck in deep sand or high-centered halfway into a ditch, a few modifications or extra equipment incorporated beforehand can mean hours or days of difference in getting the vehicle unstuck. The most expensive modification is a built-in winch, operating from the vehicle's engine or battery. The winch cable usually passes through the front or rear bumper and is attached to a secure rock, tree trunk, or land anchor set for the purpose of pulling the vehicle (or another vehicle) out of the problem area. Winches cost hundreds of dollars to purchase and install, and a lever action "come-along" or hand winch will do the same job (albeit much slower) at a fraction of the price. A come-along is also very useful on the archaeological project site or around the field site, and, not being permanently attached to the vehicle can be transported to different locations as the need arises. If a come-along is to be used to pull a stuck vehicle free of mud, sand, or silt, or off a high-center ridge, it must be attached to an easily accessible part of the vehicle's frame. If towing balls are installed at front and rear of the vehicle, the problem has been solved. If not, towing hooks (preferably with spring-loaded safety keepers) can be bolted or welded to the side of the frame or to the bumpers.

Efficiency

The first modification usually required to improve the efficiency of an archaeological field vehicle is to increase its effective operating range. If the field project location can only be reached by many hours of driving over poor roads or if the project is in a country with few filling stations, an oversize or extra fuel tanks will need to be installed. The average pickup truck or four-wheel drive vehicle has a fuel tank capacity of between 17 and 22 gallons. If it is run in compound low or four-wheel drive for protracted periods of time, 20 gallons of gas may not last for much more than 100 miles of travel. Since low gear is usually necessary in isolated areas with difficult terrain, gas consumption will be markedly greater than on good surfaces where higher gears can be used, and 5 extra gallons in a jerrycan will not make much of a difference if one runs out of gas 75 miles away from the nearest pump. Steel jerycans are also prone to leakage, to theft, and vandalism, and a good deal of waste occurs every time they are filled or discharged.

Increasing the fuel capacity of the field vehicle usually takes one of two forms; either a single, large tank is used to replace the original tank, or a pair of underslung saddle tanks are added to the original. Each system has certain advantages. The single tank incorporates only one filler cap and little gas-line rerouting, while the triple tank system necessitates three separate filler caps, installation of a tank selector switch, and fuel line rerouting. The triple tank system, however, allows for the transport of nonvehicular fuel (i.e., diesel, kerosene, pre-mixed outboard fuel, etc.) in a tank not currently in use and thus eliminates the need for filling and moving drums around, and it also allows for greater economy if a "low octane" tank is switched to a "high octane" tank only when the vehicle is under a heavy load or climbing a hill under strain. With the triple tank system, cleaning is simplified if one tank becomes contaminated by water or impurities in the fuel. Oversized or extra fuel tanks should be made of steel and should be permanently secured to the vehicle's frame and protected from accidental punctures. Plastic tanks should be avoided, for they are more prone to perforation than are metal ones, and will melt and explode if the vehicle is unavoidably driven over a flaming object. Oversize tanks should be protected by skid plates or at least by a long bar running parallel to the wheelbase of the vehicle, and should not descend below the lowest part of the frame or body. Twin saddle tanks can hold up to 26 additional gallons, while single oversize tanks can be installed with capacities of over 50 gallons.

Moving from the fuel system to the lubrication and cooling systems, some modifications can be made that will greatly extend vehicle life-expectancy and eliminate the need for mechanical attention in the field. Certain vehicles (such as older Volkswagen buses) have no replaceable oil filters of any kind, while others (such as BMC engines installed in small utility trucks and cars) have oil filters encased inside metal containers that must be disassembled prior to changing; neither is acceptable in a field vehicle. Any engine not set up for the standard kind of spin-on oil filter should be adapted to this system (conversion kits are available through J. C. Whitney of Chicago and other parts suppliers) because spin-on filters have many inherent advantages. First, over 90 percent of all spin-on filters on the market have the same thread pattern, and almost any filter can be used in an emergency until the specific one for the vehicle can be obtained. Second, the ease of replacement allows for regular changes at set intervals, which is important for protecting the engine's oil circulation system and will greatly prolong its useful life.

An engine oil cooler that can be tapped into the oil circulation system at the filter is a very good investment if the field vehicle is going to be operating constantly in temperatures over 100° F, or towing equipment or trailers in mountainous areas. The cooler itself should be mounted in front of the radiator so that the fan will work directly upon it. If the vehicle is to be operating in extremely cold climates, with the temperature below freezing much of the time, an oil heater should be considered or an engine water heater. These keep the water temperature in the block above freezing when the vehicle is parked; both, unfortunately, require constant electric current and cannot be used in the field without large batteries or generators. The oil heater usually takes the form of a "hot" dipstick that can be inserted in the normal dipstick tube. The water heater is installed in-line with the vehicle's regular heater hoses and is plugged into an AC house circuit. A cracked block or extruded freeze plugs may result if such modifications are not made in cold weather areas.

If the engine overheats in normal use, a heavy-duty fan (one with more blades than the original) can often solve the problem. Electric fans are to be avoided at all costs, for a simple short circuit in the fan system can destroy the entire engine from overheating and seizure. Cooling problems can often be solved by replacement of the existing thermostat, and in any case it should be checked periodically.

One of the most important yet often neglected modifications for field vehicles deals with instrumentation. Gauges provide an early warning system that monitors the health of the engine and allows for the diagnosis of problems as they develop. In rough terrain or in countries where spare parts and mechanics are scarce, gauges are essential. Any kind of engine repair done in the field will be greatly simplified with the help of permanently installed diagnostic instrumentation, and most troubleshooting can be done without expensive or unavailable garage-type meters. The warning or "idiot" lights that are standard equipment on most vehicles should not be relied on as they only alert the driver to the existence of a problem after it is too late to do anything about it. Moreover, there is no way to determine whether it is the system being "reported" on or the "idiot" light itself (or its circuitry) that is malfunctioning. A light will sometimes come on because of an internal short instead of a drop of oil pressure or generator failure, and, conversely, a blown bulb will not herald the lack of oil pressure that can lead to a thrown rod or blowing a piston up through the hood.

Most vehicles have a fuel gauge and speedometer as standard equipment. The field vehicle should have, in addition, an oil pressure gauge, a water temperature gauge, an ammeter, and a tachometer. A vacuum gauge tapped into the intake manifold is a useful item to have but not essential. Two options for extra gauge installation exist: many vehicles have blank spaces or empty recesses on the dashboards that can accept gauges if these originally were offered as optional equipment, or failing this, gauges can be mounted in a plate, bracket, or console that is bolted to or suspended under the dashboard. In the first situation, used gauges can usually be purchased in a wrecking yard or ordered from the parts supplier as an option; in the latter case, aftermarket gauges can be installed. Since gauges are worthless if they are not readily visible, be certain to test their location before permanent installation and to purchase models with lights that can be spliced into the existing dashlights.

Gasoline or diesel consumption is a major concern off-road or in foreign countries, especially where fuel is scarce or prohibitively expensive, and some inexpensive modifications can be made to some vehicles which will greatly improve fuel economy. If the vehicle comes standard with a three-speed transmission, the substitution of either a used four-speed or the addition of an overdrive unit may be possible. The additional gear (which may be 1:1 in the former instance and up to .7:1 in the latter) will ensure that the engine revs lower than before at any given speed in that gear, and that up to a 25 percent fuel saving will be gained, especially on long-distance hauls. Overdrive units, if bought new, are quite expensive, but used transmissions can often be purchased for $100 or so. If the engine is equipped with an overlarge carburetor (i.e.: a four-barrel instead of a two-barrel, or one with large jets instead of small), a smaller one can be installed that will draw less gasoline for no appreciable power loss except in rapid acceleration; jackrabbit starts are usually not necessary in the field, and the switch to a "gas-saver" carburetor can often improve mileage from 2 to 8 miles per gallon. Dual exhaust pipes and mufflers if the vehicle is a V-8 will also improve horsepower at no appreciable increase in gas consumption and thus actually create a saving in fuel, as will the substitution of a manual choke for an automatic choke on most carburetors. A properly functioning electrical system and correct timing is crucial for good fuel economy, and all timing specifications such as point and plug gap, plug type, timing in degrees before top dead center, and so forth should be adhered to after experimentation provides the best settings. Cleaning the crankshaft pulley, and painting it a bright color, then painting the timing marks bright or fluorescent white, will simplify timing chores while stranded in tropical streams over the axles or while mired in desert sands during midnight sciroccos. So will numbering the spark plug wires by either painting the cylinder numbers on the distributor cap or by slipping numbered sleeves on the leads themselves, and by inspecting the leads for faults. Plugs that are too hot or too cold for the engine not only ensure poor performance but also contribute to miserable fuel economy; some experimentation with different heat ranges may be necessary before the correct plug is discovered.

The most important modifications for obtaining the greatest distance of travel per liter or gallon of gasoline lie in changes that can be made to the vehicle's power-to-weight ratio and in the reduction of certain kinds of engine strain. Two vehicles with identical engines but with different laden weights can be expected to get very different mpg ratings, as will two vehicles identical in all respects except for the pressence of power-robbing "extras" in one of them. An 800 pound hi-rise camper mounted on a pickup truck can decrease fuel efficiency by around 20 to 30 percent over a low-profile lightweight camper shell; and 300 unnecessary pounds of safety glass such as can be found in "carryall" type vehicles are going to make much more of a difference to gas consumption than will a lightweight fiberglass or aluminum skin covering a pickup bed.

Many maintenance and repair problems that develop in field vehicles are rare or unheard of in street vehicles, and most of these are due to constant road shocks and vibration. Nuts and bolts are constantly working loose and shaking or falling off, assemblies abrade against each other and wiring develops shorts from being pinched between moving parts; I have even had an entire carburetor shake loose and fall off an engine in the field because of excessive vibration. The point being made here is that the smoother the ride, the less wear and tear on the vehicle and less corrective surgery needs to be done. Springs can be raised so as to improve clearance through installing shackles or lift blocks, and oversize tires and wheels can then be installed. Helpers or dampers can be bolted to leaf springs so as to stiffen them, and air bags inside coil springs will improve their performance also. Shock absorbers are crucial in eliminating vibration and its concomitant damage to the vehicle, and many off-road supply companies offer kits that allow for the installation of double shock absorbers, or pneumatic (air) versions. The heavier the vehicle, generally, the more important it is to choose shock absorbers for field use. Worn or weak shocks will adversely affect tire life, front-end alignment and fuel consumption, not to mention the discomfort they will cause to the passengers. If excessive play develops in the steering system, or road shocks threaten to break fingers caught in the spokes of steering wheels, a steering stabilizer (or damper) may be necessary. Normal adjustment can usually, however, take up excessive slack or "play" in the system and stiffen it.

Less common and more abstruse modifications may be necessary in order to prepare a specific vehicle for a specific kind of project. In extremely swampy areas, for example, it might be considered necessary to waterproof the electrical system by covering the distributor, generator, spark plugs, and so forth with rubber "boots" and to install high-stake exhausts so as to avoid inundating the exhaust valves. Or, if the vehicle is to be used as an ambulatory photographic platform, a flat deck may be installed above the roof with permanent sockets for camera tripods and safety boxes for film. For use on ice or snow, it may be desirable to convert the vehicle to a half-track with the addition of a second (non-powered) set of wheels and axle, or to substitute skis for the front wheels; the list could obviously go on and on, and the point here is that modifications are endless in their variability of application.

Conclusion

This article was not written with the intent of urging archaeologists to stop doing archaeology and become inveterate hotrodders or slaves to their machinery. It does suggest, however, that one of the most important research investments any archaeologist can make is in his or her basic transportation. There is no reason why a carefully selected, properly maintained and protected field vehicle cannot be expected to serve faithfully for twenty years or more and to provide transportation for many successive generations of archaeologists. Because archaeologists are very much the low men on the scientific totem pole as regards academic funding, they must expend their budgets judiciously and with the expectation that major equipment items should outlast the successive coursework investments of the students who use them. Unfortunately, it is sometimes a paradox of inexplicable nature that the archaeologist who will not let a D- student near a $1500.00 alidade will nevertheless send the same person off in the $1500.00 project vehicle. If the archaeologist does not know how to rescue the vehicle from a breakdown situation, he certainly should not expect the student to know either, and can only blame himself if things go wrong.

Earlier generations of archaeologists and ethnologists, used to horse and buggy travel, welcomed the motor vehicle as a logistical godsend; most of these individuals learned as a matter of course to do basic mechanical repair and were capable of getting out of any hole they got into. In order to do fieldwork, such researchers thought nothing of camping "for two or three days in a roadside ditch while I reconstructed the car motor, replacing a broken valve head and piston" (Beals 1982: 6), but many present students and professionals would not dream of solving such problems themselves today. Those few individuals who take the plunge and come to know vehicular problems and solutions as well as any mechanic will find such information easy to obtain, and priceless in field situations. They will also find that it will contribute in large measure to the logistical smoothness of their operation and ultimately to the success of their projects.

ARCHAEOLOGICAL SURVEY VIA MULE-BACK

Thomas J. Banks and Brian D. Dillon

Introduction

Mules left lasting impressions with many early field archaeologists in the Americas (both literally and figuratively) and most expeditions during the discipline's formative years were mule-powered. Even today some researchers depend upon mules as a solution of their basic transportation and supply problems, but this tradition is nowhere near as well developed in the United States as it is in most Latin American countries. Because the mule never became popular in Great Britain, English-speaking colonists in the Americas tended to have an inborn predjudice against the animal until at least as late as the Revolutionary War, when George Washington himself popularized the breed in the new nation (Howard, 1965). In contrast, the mule had been appreciated and sought after in Latin America (including those territories later to become part of the United States) since Columbus' third voyage in 1498 and quickly became the most important European draft animal to replace human bearers.

The crucial trans-isthmian route across Panama which essentially linked all of Pacific Middle and South America with the Spanish motherland was entirely dependent upon mules for its operation by as early as 1550, and entire provinces in the New World were turned over to mule-breeding ranches so as to keep supply in pace with demand. The mineral and metal prospecting that stimulated so much of the exploration and exploitation of the New World was also mule-powered, and at times entire regions devoted all non-mining activities such as stock-raising towards the end of supplying mining ventures with enough animals to keep loads of ore moving to the refiners. The Choluteca area of Pacific coastal Honduras, for example, has specialized in breeding mules as is basic "export crop" for something over 400 years (Mac Leod, 1973) and animals with such pedigrees are ideal for archaelog ses.

Mules are the offspring of a male donkey (an ass or burro) and a female horse (or mare). The progeny can be either male (a jack) or female (a jenny) but is invariably sterile. Consequences of genetic hybridism endow mules with superiorities over either parent and make him more suitable than his progenitors as either a mount or as a draft or pack animal. Compared with horses, mules are generally longer lived, more disease-resistant, more intelligent, have greater stamina, pulling or carrying power, and require much less maintenance.

Early archaeological explorers in the New World almost to a man were mule-borne, as their forays took place long before the introduction of the motor vehicle and in some cases before the invention or spread of steam railway lines. Nevertheless, it should be remembered that these researchers could have gone by foot or horse, yet chose not to. Travelers quickly found that in many locations, the only way to get from their starting point to their destination was by mule and no other way would do. One of the earliest passages in the four-volume series of travel books penned by John L. Stephens (1841, vol. 1: 43) relates to his first few days in the Guatemalan Republic during the rainy season of 1839: "The woods were of impenetrable thickness; and there was no view except that of the detestable path before us. For five long hours we were dragged through mudholes, squeezed in gulleys, knocked against trees, and tumbled over roots; every step required care and great physical exertion; and, withal, I felt that our inglorious epitaph might be, "tossed over the head of a mule, brained by the trunk of a mahogany-tree, and buried in the mud of the Mico Mountain." One of us can attest that the horrors of mule travel during the Guatemalan rainy season had changed not a whit by 1975 and will likely continue to be as unpleasant for some time to come. The alternative to mule travel, in this case, of course, is simply staying at home.

Besides their ability to go where most pedestrians would fear to tread, mules have the wonderful quality of being able to subsist on very poor feed or go without for long stretches of time. Christian Barthelmess, a German-born U.S. Army musician turned part-time ethnographic photographer on the Great Plains and in the Southwest, commented after a 450-mile mule ride to the Grand Canyon in 1887, "Most of my readers no doubt are acquainted with the common, everyday mule, *Mulus communis,* as he is found roaming throughout the Western states, and know how, in case of total absence of his regular diet, he can subsist on fence posts, barbed wire, old tin cans, newspapers, and theater tickets: (Frink and Barthelmess 1965:64-65).

Besides being able to work day after day with only a pittance of feed that would prove deadly to a horse, mules can also withstand a high level of abuse and occasionally work under very adverse conditions (qualities the field archaeologist sometimes feels are his own exclusive preserve). The mule's ability to endure hard work and privation made him a logical choice as a Christian exemplar of good conduct in the popular *Lessons from the Animal World* a century-and-a-half ago: "At Paraguay, [Jack] asses are treated with great cruelty. No food nor shelter is found for them, and young persons are allowed to maim and ill-treat them as a matter of amusement. A favourite trick of these barbarians is to cut and split open the ears of the poor animals, so that it is very rare to meet with an ass having both ears perfect" (Tomlinson and Tomlinson 1845 [1859]:197). Paraguay, of course, was not unique among nations for this kind of abuse, and many a mule has found itself more easily handled by an archaeologist than ever before or after in its life.

A mule can get by with less and go farther than a horse can, and an additional advantage is its innate sense of caution, patience, and muscular control. A horse, if panicked, will easily damage itself (and, coincidentally, its rider as well), but mules almost never stampede over cliffs or eviscerate themselves on tree-trunks. The commonly applied adjective "sure-footed" would seem to best characterize mules in this light, but perhaps more apropos would be "cold and calculating." While mules

Figure 1: The quadrupedal half of an archaeological field survey. Saddle mules loaded with camping gear, clearing tools, and recording equipment, near Chinaja, Alta Verapaz, Guatemala, 1975.

may be sure-footed, they are also intelligent enough to know when sacrificing their rider or their cargo will provide them an advantage of comfort or safety, and they usually do not hesitate to do either. Robert Wauchope (1974:7-9) provides a wonderful account of his introduction to both Maya archaeology with the Carnegie Institution over fifty years ago and to the American tropical rain forest: "The first day we were in the saddle ten hours, not one minute of which could be called relaxed riding...All day long we tore through unbushed side trails, wallowed in mud up to the mules' bellies, were lashed by vines and ripped by thorns. Even the mules, in which I had placed an unwarranted confidence, lost their footing, stumbled, or fell sprawling and kicking in apparent panic. We frequently held our booted legs out of the stirrups, high on the mule's neck, in order to leap clear if the animal fell or to avoid being crushed against the spiny tree trunks along the side of the trail. Time and again we had to cut the floundering mules clear of vines and lift them bodily from mudholes."

Things have changed but little in the Maya area, and often times crafty or mean Peten mules will still select a spiny *escoba* palm trunk just off the trail to jam its unsuspecting rider's leg against, or will wait for a sense of somnambulance on the part of the rider and for the deepest puddle before flipping him off head-first into the mud. Any mule in its right mind will try to rid itself of an unbalanced or overweight pack, and favorite tricks are rubbing it against low branches or ramming it against rocks at a full run; perhaps the most effective routine is to roll over and over until the pack and all of its contents are pulverized. The archaeologist inbound with a mule-mounted transit or outbound with pottery vessels or osteological materials would do well to control his mule with as much attention as he would devote to a bottle of nitroglycerine, or else disaster is certain to occur. The mule can usually be persuaded into co-operating through the judicious administration of edible bribes, or coerced through the application of a switch or club to its hindquarters.

Practical Applications

If the foregoing discussion has served to convince the incipient archaeological explorer that mules are a necessity in many places south of the border, it nevertheless bypasses the point that in the United States few places remain that cannot be reached by some form of motorized transport. We are left with the question, Why use a mule to conduct archaeological surveys in this country? The answer is fairly obvious: while you may use a dirt bike, jeep, or other off-road vehicle to get to the region to be reconnoitered, you would hardly "drive transects" a few meters apart in search of surface scatters, lithic accumulations, and so forth, because of the likelihood of destruction to those archaeological deposits and because more attention needs to be devoted to running the vehicle than to looking for artifacts. Site survey from muleback, however, produces none of these disadvantages, and most people would certainly rather ride than walk if the archaeological reconnaissance incorporates hundreds or thousands of acres of land.

In many cases the ability to visually locate artifacts improves with the archaeologist's mounted state. If the investigator has average vision, his horizontal range of ground visibility is greater in the saddle than it is on foot, simply because the eye has been elevated several additional feet. An archaeologist in the saddle can locate flakes, beads, and other small objects reasonably well from this distance (approximately 6 to 8 feet) and can always dismount and engage in a closer inspection if presented with an equivocal situation. To avoid constant mounting and dismounting, the mule-borne archaeologist may find it helpful to keep a pair of low-power binoculars with him to scan likely areas immediately below.

One rider with the aid of one mule can survey approximately 200 acres of brushy hillside in a day, riding transect intervals of 20 meters or so. A leather breast guard is fastened to the mule that is going to plow through very dense brush "icebreaker fashion," to protect it from possible injury and give it greater confidence. In less difficult terrain, such as flat, clear ground, a single rider can easily reconnoiter 400 to 500 acres in a day. Thirty-meter wide transects can be ridden in open country because of the increased visibility from the saddle, and this enables the surveyor to cover more ground.

Mishaps can occur during such surveys, usually when least expected. One of us was doing a reconnaissance of a stretch of desert one day when a piece of jumping cholla became imbedded in the mule's underside. Unknowingly, the intentional action of the stirrup accidentally drove the cholla spines deeper into the mount, and the mule's reaction was to take off at a gallop which was only terminated by the unfortunate appearance of a rabbit burrow. The mule tripped, and threw both itself and its rider into the middle of the largest cholla located during the entire survey; it took a veterinarian and two assistants the remainder of the day to extract the resulting spines with tweezers, and the vet's fee obviated any profit from the enterprise.

A selection of nearly forty survey projects incorporating approximately 43,797 acres completed by one of us (Banks) on muleback is listed in Table 1; these data demonstrate the very good cost-efficiency of mule surveys which improves dramatically as the acreage involved increases. Some archaeologists, however, are skeptical about the success or even suitability of muleback surveys, and questions range from; Can you really see the ground from up there? to; Won't the mule eat rare plants? In areas overpopulated by free-lance archaeologists, such as Southern California, some individuals have cautioned that increased efficiency of the mule survey system will put other fieldworkers on the unemployment line. Most of the archaeological resistance to the idea of riding a mule to the project location or riding a mule at the project location to locate archaeological sites has, in fact, little to do with theoretical concerns about efficiency or cost-effectiveness. The real reason for the mulish attitude shown by many archaeologists is a fear of the animals themselves or a total lack of equestrian experience, either of which can result in feeling ridiculous or insecure once in the saddle.

Despite our sometimes gruesome accounts of 19th century mule travel (and those peculiar to the rain forest), archaeologists have nothing to fear from properly broken mule. Once a relationship has been established, and the rider convinces the mule that he can expect affection and good treatment, the animal will usually become more of a friend and partner than logistical adjunct. No vehicle, for example, could ever be told to walk straight lines all day while its driver takes notes, reads maps, takes photographs, and generally does everything except use his hands to control the direction of travel, yet any well-trained mule will go exactly where his rider wants him to go.

Critics of muleback surveys who cite lack of efficiency in comparison with foot surveys should do well to study the results of an experiment carried out on September 22, 1979 (Table 3), in which one of us was pitted on muleback against an on-foot survey crew of four, both charged with surveying the same 90-acre parcel. The mule and rider took 4 hours to reconnoiter the area, while the on-foot crew expended 24 man-hours; the mule and rider not only located every site originally found by the on-foot crew but also discovered additional archaeological sites that were missed by the other crew. Best of all, the rider concluded his survey with reserves of energy left, ready to do archaeology, while the on-foot crew was exhausted from nonarchaeological exertions (such as walking, climbing, and so forth).

Other archaeological survey made from horseback in California and Nevada are listed in Table 2. A much more audacious project is that of Crosby (1974) who has traced the route of the old King's Road through most of the Baja California peninsula by mule, and who has used mules in the localization of archaeological sites in this difficult country (1975).

Preparations

It is highly recommended that the archaeologist intending to work with mules in a far-off country or region gain some familiarity with the creatures close to home before leaving. In many places mules are not available but horses are, and in general all rules applying to the care of, riding, and training of horses apply equally to mules. Since mules are more tolerant of their rider's or packer's shortcomings, it makes particular good sense to learn the business with horses first, for no problems will seem insurmountable with mules once the tricks of horses have been mastered. Any riding stable will be more than happy to instruct the novice in the rudiments of riding, feeding, and setting up the saddle and bridle, but there are few

Table 1: Mule-Borne Archaeological Surveys in Western North America, 1979–1981.

SIX-MONTH LISTING OF MULE BORNE SURVEYS (1979)*

DATE	LOCATION	SITES LOCATED	TOTAL ACRES	ACRES/DAY
July **	Julian, CA	15 (+ 2 isolates)	2600	260
August	Thousand Oaks, CA	2	1500	375
September	Riverside, CA	2	600	300
September	Jacumba, CA	(reliability test: 15)	90	90
September	Santa Ysabel, CA	2	650	217
October	Thousand Oaks, CA	13	5400	270
November	Desert Hot Springs, CA	0	540	270
November	Riverside, CA	21	1485	187
December	Walnut, CA	3	540	180
December	Thousand Palms, CA	0	200	200
December	Tehachapi, CA	4 (+ 1 isolate)	1900	380
December	Gustine, CA	5 (+ 2 isolates)	1840	230

MULE-BORNE SURVEYS IN 1980

DATE	LOCATION	SITES LOCATED	TOTAL ACRES	ACRES/DAY
January	Otay Valley, CA	4	250	250
February	Riverside, CA	1	300	300
February	Santee, CA	0	100	100
February	San Diego, CA	1	75	75
February	Live Oak Canyon, CA	0	200	200
March	Valley Center, CA	1	50	50
April	Valley Center, CA	0	80	80
April-June	Eastern North Dakota	40	8000	400
June	Poway, CA	0	40	40
June	Escondido, CA	0	40	40
July	Temecula, CA	0	1000	500
August	Sun City, CA	1	600	300
September	Rancho, CA	3	800	270
October	Sun City, CA	6	1800	600
October	Jacumba, CA	3	180	180
October	Oakzanita, CA	3	110	110
November	Jacumba, CA	7	585	260

MULE-BORNE SURVEYS IN 1981

DATE	LOCATION	SITES LOCATED	TOTAL ACRES	ACRES/DAY
February	Murrieta, CA	6	2000	300
February	Tehachapi, CA	27	5990	400
March	San Pascual, CA	3	900	300
April	Diamond Bar, CA	2	360	360
May	Temecula, CA	4	700	180
June	Lake Elsinore, CA	1	600	200

* All surveys conducted by T.J. Banks.
** First survey conducted.

places the archaeological practicioner can go in order to learn how to pack and un-pack mules, and even fewer published sources on the subject.

If the student can afford it, an extended trip into the back country will expose animal-handling novices to the problems and solutions of pack mule use, but most archaeologists cannot afford either the cost or the investment of time that is necessary in order to learn basic packing techniques. Relatively complete written guides do exist, however, in a number of older military publications; the *Drill Regulations for Field Companies of the Signal Corps* for 1911, for example, is devoted mainly to proper equestrian technique, pack saddle loading, and stable management. The archaeologist residing upon an urban campus with little opportunity to practice mule-handling before venturing into the field is well advised to review the technical literature on the subject, for fewer broken bones and lost collections will result. The rudiments of loading and unloading, feeding, doctoring and riding can also, of course, be learned first with horses and then later transferred to mules. In fact, the archaeologist who finds himself only moderately successful in adapting horses to archaeological purposes in a simulated context may be pleased to discover that he excells with mules in practical field application.

Riding a mule is not much different from riding a horse; mules will, however, tolerate a greater level of abuse than their more high-strung consanguineous counterparts. Packhorses show very poorly in comparison with even the smallest packmules, on the other hand, and efficiency can often be improved by 100% through utilizing the latter over the former. It is very important to set up the pack saddle correctly and to load it properly, so that the cargo is secure and the mule is comfortable and willing to carry his or her load. On large, North American ("Missouri" type) mules, pack loads of up to 250 pounds can be accomodated, but throughout other areas, such as Latin America, where mules are comparatively smaller and are often undernourished, such loads result in immediate mutiny and disaster. An overweight rider will often, in such contexts, find him or herself flying towards the ground because the mule cannot withstand his weight.

Although not always done on short hauls, the mule should be unloaded at the end of each day and his back (where the load or saddle was positioned) should be rubbed down. This practice is recommended not so much to provide the pack animal with a period of rest and comfort as it is to allow inspection of his back so that swelling or sores can be medicated. Such afflictions are painful to the mule and can adversely affect his humor and efficiency. Sores result from three different conditions: the cinch or *apareja* is too tight, the pack saddle is too loose and is moving too much, or a portion of the saddle or the load is pressing harder or more sharply into the mule's back than the other portions are. Salve should always be carried so that sores can be attended to immediately, and in extreme cases it may be necessary to halt travel for a day or two so that healing can commence. When loading and unloading the mule, special care should be taken to ensure that the pad is clean and dry; otherwise dirt, sand, bark or twigs clinging to it will abrade the mule's back and cause sores.

Renting or Buying

Arguments both for and against hiring your own *arriero* and a few mules for a short time should be considered before a decision is made. Hiring the mule's owner along with the animals relieves the archaeologist of the tedium of daily packing and unpacking, and frees more time for actual archaeology. If a mule gets sick, or dies, it is the owner's problem (who is there on the scene) and not the archaeologist's; when the animals bolt or stray, it is the muleskinner who must chase them, not the field

Table 2: Recent Equestrian (Horse) Surveys, Western North America.

DATE	LOCATION	SURVEY BY
March-May, 1976	Lander's County, Nevada; 15.25 miles^2, 7 isolated finds located.	Dr. Roberta McGonagle, BLM Archaeologist, Battle Mountain District Office, Nevada
November, 1977	Santa Maria River Bed, 17 mile stretch for levee improvement near Ventura, California. No sites.	Patricia Martz, Archaeologist, US Army Corps of Engineers, Los Angeles, California
November-December, 1977	Lander's County, Nevada; 73 acres of proposed fence line, 3 sites and 3 isolated finds located.	Dr. Roberta McGonagle, BLM Archaeologist, Battle Mountain District Office, Nevada
May, 1978	Lander's County, Nevada; 5 miles along a proposed fence line, 6 sites located.	" "
March-April, 1978	Nye County, Nevada; 85 miles of proposed fench line, 11 sites and 12 isolates discovered.	" "
June, 1978	Nye County, Nevada; 6.2 miles of proposed fence line; 1 site and 2 isolates located.	" "
June, 1978	Nye County, Nevada; 5 miles of proposed fence line, 1 site located.	" "
June, 1978	Nye County, Nevada; 3 miles of proposed fence line, 3 sites located.	" "

Table 3: Comparison between an on-foot (left) and a mule-borne (right) archaeological survey of the same 90-acre plot near Jacumba, California.

C-143 (roasting pits, flakes)	J-1, 14, 15
none	J-2 (roasting pit)
none	J-3 (coring area)
C-415 (roasting pit, flakes)	J-4 (no flakes found)
B-1, 2, 3	J-5 (flakes, no pits)
none	J-6 (roasting pit)
C-416, 418	J-8
C-416 (roasting pit)	J-9
none	J-10
none	J-11
C-414 (roasting pits)	J-12
none	J-13 (one flake)
none	J-14 (one flake)
C-413 (roasting pit, pottery)	J-15
May-6 (flake and coring area)	J-16
C-411 (milling feature, flakes)	J-17
C-394 (flaking area)	J-18
NA-2 (campsite, flakes)	J-19
D-2 (rockshelter, milling area, flakes)	J-20
C-1 (rancheria)	J-21
NA-1 (milling area, flakes)	J-22

Notes: The on-foot crew numbered four persons, and 24 man-hours were invested in their survey. The mule-borne survey (by Banks) took four man hours on mule back. Seven sites or archaeological locations missed by the on-foot crew were discovered by the mule-borne survey, in only 1/6th the time expended.

researcher. The mule's owner, however, often exerts a limiting influence on the progress of the project, for an overly cautious *arriero* may baulk at the route the archaeologist has chosen, demand that his mules be driven less hard or less long, and even claim that one of his animals is sick when in fact it is he that is tired of travelling or of working. Renting mules is, of course, more economical than buying them if a short-term field project is planned, and all the gear necessary (saddle, bridle, etc.) usually accompanies the animal as part of the rental. The rentor does not have to cover the expense of providing feed and medicine for the mule when it is not in actual use, and suffers no capital loss if it sickens or dies after the term of rental has expired.

Archaeologists planning to use mules constantly may find it more economical to buy one or two animals, use them for a season, and then to recover part of their investment by selling them off at the season's end. The purchase price will almost always be greater than the selling price (which may be ridiculously low, especially in foreign countries); indeed, the archaeologist can never prove that his animal is not at death's door to a potential purchaser, and is only good for the glue factory. If the price offered is offensive or ridiculous, the archaeologist can always make a present of the mule to a trusted foreman or workman and arrange for its use on a loan basis the next season. It should also be remembered that buying mules is a dead-end investment, for since they cannot procreate, no additional return can be expected as is the case with horses and donkeys.

While in Latin America a pack or saddle mule complete with rig may cost only two or three dollars a day to rent and a few hundred dollars to purchase, in North America a good riding mule may cost dozens of dollars to hire and well over a thousand to buy. A good used saddle in this country will cost around 200 dollars; pack saddles will of course be much cheaper or can be constructed by the archaeologist himself. Saddle bags will run about 30 dollars; bit, bridle, and reins will total around 100 dollars. Two saddle blankets should cost no more than 50 dollars, and lead rope and halter, hobbles, and nose bag should total out at around 33 dollars. Chaps and other riding gear can cost up to 100 dollars, and the total investment can easily run to around 2,000 dollars.

A horse trailer rents for approximately 20 dollars per day but can be purchased for around 2,500 dollars second-hand. If the archaeologist does not have the land to stable the mule, boarding fees average around 100 dollars per month. Shoeing costs around 30 dollars every six weeks, and worming consumes 20 dollars annually. Other costs involve purchase or running expense for the vehicle used to pull the horse trailer, and unexpected veterinarian's fees. It would seem that from the preceding discussion, 99 archaeologists out of 100 would do better to rent mules than to buy them, but this decision is properly left to each individual and to the needs of his or her specific project.

Conclusions

The archaeologist who uses mules obtains a practical advantage over the one who relies on motorized transport in many situations, and over on-foot surveyors in open or brushy country almost without exception. We have noted that a century and a half ago, nearly all archaeological projects depended to a greater or a lesser extent on mule-power, yet that almost nobody today considers the mule essential equipment. Unfortunately, as fewer and fewer archaeologists today come to have any rural background, we predict that mule use in archaeology will become even more of a novelty, at least in this country. We are confident, on the other hand, that in many parts of the world where motor vehicles have not yet made inroads as profound as in North America, archaeologists and mules will enjoy productive associations for many years to come.

SMALL BOATS IN ARCHAEOLOGICAL EXPLORATION

Clement W. Meighan and Brian D. Dillon

Introduction

Archaeologists have written little about small boats as a logistical aid to field research, even though such use has been widespread within the discipline for more than a century and a half. Boats are not generally discussed because of the common and substantially incorrect assumption that field archaeologists will naturally select the best transportation medium available. While many, if not most, field archaeologists feel that they have a reasonable facility with land travel, few devote much thought or planning to water transportation. Indeed, informal quizzing of associates over the years has led us to conclude that most archaeologists avoid water transport even in situations where such aid could provide the field researcher with a distinct logistical advantage over other possibilities and save the project much time and cost.

It seems that resistance to the idea of using small boats in archaeological exploration projects or for basic transportation originates with the landsman's position that water is an obstacle to travel; the boatman's basic view, of course, is that water is a means of facilitating travel. We suggest that it is time that archaeologists become more attuned to the particulars of small boat operation, for this will result in increased efficiency in field projects. Recently one of us directed a project in Pacific Central America in which a small boat was used daily as the chief means of supplying a field camp and excavation several kilometers away across open water. This often meant that the project leader had to spend up to eight or nine hours a day just running the boat because almost without exception other project members were incapable of doing so. It was remarkable to see how unfamiliar most were with boats and with water safety; even those who were experts on the archaeology of the nearby coastline were as unaccustomed to operating a boat as they would have been to piloting an aircraft and were constantly committing major and minor blunders that could have had serious consequences under more adverse sea and weather conditions.

Early archaeological travelers and explorers in the New World were accustomed to using whatever form of transportation was available, either familiar (horse, mule, railway coach) or unfamiliar (pack-llamas, dugout canoes, balsas, etc.), and often these intrepid souls were taking something of a risk. Many archaeologists are familiar with John L. Stephens's account of almost drowning in Lake Atitlan in a dugout canoe (1841,2: 162-163) and with Ephraim George Squier's account of voyaging in search of monumental sculpture on the islands of Lake Nicaragua in 1849, which was accomplished by obtaining "one of their *bongos* . . . the largest and most comfortable on the lake; and as most of this kind of unique craft are only gigantic canoes, hollowed from a single trunk of the cebia [sic], and quite as well fitted, and just as much disposed, to sail upon their sides or bottom up as any other way, it was a gratification to know that 'La Carlota' had been built with something of a keel..." (1852: 43). Since this time many other archaeologists have found that small boats provide the best (and in some circumstances, the only) way to get to their project location.

A surprising number of archaeological sites are accessible only by water; a still larger number exist for which access by water is far more practical than attempting to reach them overland. These include riverine locations, sites along shorelines backed by dense vegetation, sites in marshy areas or in zones surrounded by mangrove swamps, and shoreline sites at the base of steep cliffs. Both the discovery and excavation of such sites may not be possible using conventional land-based transportation, or possible only after great expenditures of resources. Omitted from this discussion are underwater archaeological sites, be they the result of geological subsidence or of some historical maritime misadventure, for we assume that every nautical archaeologist has as his or her most basic accomplishment a familiarity with boats and boating. The terrestrial archaeologist, however, is used to solving logistical problems through the use of motor vehicles or draft animals and finds the going difficult in the absence of roads, mules, or the means of getting fuel to the field camp or vehicle. Unfortunately, when faced with the decision of abandoning plans for a project or shifting to a boat-based solution of logistical problems, he may not always consider boats a viable solution and may not stop to consider the practical advantages of boats over "going the long way around" and clearing miles of trail or building miles of road.

An extremely helpful account of the kinds of problems the archaeologist has to face in difficult field situations is provided by Meggers and Evans, who certainly could not have selected a more difficult location or one in which small boats could play a more important role (1957: 9-10): "In spite of all the modern mechanical aids to mankind, one is reduced to the necessity of utilizing the primitive, local means of transportation. More than once after a slow and difficult dugout trip we wished for an outboard motor, but there were many other situations in which paddling in a dugout was 100 percent more practical . . . . To use motors it is necessary to haul all the gasoline from a main base and establish caches of fuel. To do this would involve organization and planning of supplies that would be more time consuming and frustrating in the long run than the use of local transportation... Those who have never traveled in the interior of the Amazon, along the smaller streams where only a hunter, wood cutter or rubber cutter might live, sometimes find it difficult to understand the importance of the dugout as a means of transportation.... Regardless of how much planning is done beforehand or how much money one has available, there is no way to avoid traveling by foot, by horse, by bullock, by dugout, and by sailboat, even though occasionally the airplane, jeep, truck, outboard motor or launch may be thrown in for the sake of variety. In other words, the local situation cannot be predicted. One might carry an outboard motor and

Figure 1: Small boat construction, Tilapa, south coast, Guatemala, 1976. A dugout canoe (cayuco) of approximately 8 meters length, 1.5 meters beam. Note solid transverse brace left slightly forward of stern. Cayuco has vee-hulled prow and stern, flat bottomed central section. A single hardwood trunk is shaped on exterior after de-barking and blocking, then hollowed out through controlled burning and adzing. Total construction time takes 3 to 5 months for one expert, using steel tools. Such cayucos draw between 5 and 20 cm, and are powered by poles, paddles, and offset outboards. They are used for estuarine and offshore travel, and can carry up to several tons of cargo.

gasoline for weeks and then discover that the local conditions of a particular stream make use of the motor impossible, and paddling a dugout the only resort."

Some archaeologists will spend a day on the water trying to do a project and will experience so many problems or become so alarmed that they forswear small boats forever. Even more will hire a supposed expert to run the boat and will be financially victimized owing to their ignorance about what the personnel or cargo capacity of a particular boat is, how long it should take to get from point A to point B, and so forth. On one recent project that one of us was involved in, local boatmen were happy to make five trips across a body of water when one or two would have sufficed; they were, of course, being paid by the trip and were regularly charging the project up to $100.00 per day in transportation expenses. With the arrival of a more knowledgeable person, the practice was discontinued and the project's own boat with outboard motor was rented for $100.00 per month.

The present focus is on small boats for extended use, and it is presumed that the archaeologist himself will either be running the boat or directly supervising its operation. Casual use of a boat with a hired crew requires no specific knowledge on the part of the archaeologist, only an inflated wallet. We also forgo any discussion of large boats (i.e., fully-decked) and extended voyages out of sight of land, for our interest is in how small boats can logistically aid terrestrial archaeology.

Using boats in an archaeological field situation produces another advantage in any waterline area by giving the researcher a feel for the place as it appeared to its ancient inhabitants. Where boats were prehistorically important, the archaeologist by utilizing water transportation can gain essential knowledge about earlier use of the environment. This knowledge, which might otherwise not be available to him, can also lead to a better understanding of settlement patterns on shore as well as the opportunities or constraints provided by the river, lake, or ocean environment. Having some first-hand experience with boating as it was practiced by the peoples of the past may provide important insights for interpretation; at the very least it should help the archaeologist prevent imaginary or impossible scenarios from entering into his conclusions about ancient water-related activities. Some authors, for example, have reconstructed the aboriginal use of small boats under conditions where such use would have been unlikely given the known wind, current, or wave conditions. Conversely, others have entirely ignored the possibilities of ancient water-based travel or water-based economic specialization, because through their own inexperience they could not visualize such possiblities.

Ethnographers and ethnohistorians have paid much more attention to the use of boats, often using native boats, replicating them, or making boat voyages under primitive conditions to gain insight into ethnohistorical questions. Best known are the long ocean voyages of Heyerdahl and others who have repeated the experiences of presumed earlier boatmen in what most archaeologists would see as a very complex and lengthy imitative experiment. Since such voyages are essentially nonarchaeological (in that no archaeological evidence is produced or discovered), we shall not consider them in the present discussion of practical applications to archaeological endeavor.

Some studies are available on small native-made boats, and ethnographic accounts of such craft are immensely valuable when they include information about the effectiveness and efficiency of particualr designs. For example, Hudson (1981) discusses the problem of "ocean-going" dugouts in northern California, based in part on his experience with reconstructing and using one of the sea-going canoes formerly made by the Indians of Southern California. Such studies, however, are principally of value for clarifying what can and cannot be done with native boats and essential knowledge for interpreting past boat-using cultures but not terribly useful for the archaeologist contemplating a fully or partly water-based field project.

Small Boat Selection

The type of boat required for the archaeological party of two that must pack everything (including their boat) up to a mountain lake on muleback in order to explore an island will be very different than the one needed for a crew of ten which will be crossing rough water at least twice a day. The first situation calls for either a folding kayak (such as the 16-foot Klepper) or an inflatable rubber raft that can be lashed to a pack saddle, while for the second any boat other than a vee-hulled outboard or partially decked sailer with a keel would not be suitable. In most cases

Figure 2: Outboard-powered dugout canoes in use on the Rio Chixoy (or Salinas) at Rubelsanto, Alta Verapaz, Guatemala, in 1975. Note built-up gunwales on the cayuco at center, sunken one at right. Used during Salinas de los Nueve Cerros project.

fully-equipped "pleasure boats," regardless of their size, are either too heavy, draw too much water, consume too much fuel, or have too little cargo capacity to be of much use to the archaeologist and should be eschewed. The field researcher should select a "work boat" (Figure 2) of a kind used for commercial (i.e., "practical") purposes, one with a long history of success in withstanding daily use and abuse without turning into a submersible.

Perhaps the most universal of all small boats is the inflatable. The British-made Avon has come to be thought of as representative of the type (much as "Kodak" is often used synonymously for cameras), although many other makes (such as Zodiac) are equally famous. Inflatables have many advantages over conventional rigid-hulled boats. They are compact and weigh so little that they can be transported very easily while out of the water, an important consideration if air travel is to be utilized. Inflatables come in a wide variety of shapes, sizes and designs for specific kinds of motive power and functions, but all are relatively inexpensive. Cost is dependent upon size and the method of construction; lightweight toy or "swimming pool" rubber rafts, while cheapest of all, should not be considered for serious archaeological work. Disadvantages of inflatables are that they can be easily punctured or torn and thus are not as safe around rocky shorelines as rigid-hulled boats can be; also, in no other kind of craft can a dropped cigarette burn through the hull and sink

Figure 3:   20 foot-long wood and fiberglass ocean-going Pongo on the Bay of Culebra, Guanacaste, Costa Rica.   Used during the Nacascolo project, 1980-1981.

the boat. Because inflatables are flat-bottomed, they have only limited stability in heavy wind or high waves and thus tend to swamp very easily. They are easy to overpower with outboard motors and very difficult to navigate or even to keep on a straight course under muscle power. On the other hand, inflatables are easier to repair than almost any other kind of boat, for all that is needed are needle and thread, and a tube-patch kit.

In addition to inflatables, a great variety of small rigid-hulled boats are available from commercial outlets such as larger boatyards, department stores, sporting goods emporiums and the want-ads of coastal newspapers. These are constructed of wood, metal, fiberglass or a combination of such materials, and are very efficient when used appropriately under the conditions for which they were designed. Most rigid-hulled boats share at least one feature with inflatables: built-in positive flotation chambers. These are sealed air compartments (or are filled with cork or styrofoam) that can keep the boat afloat even if it fills with water. Rigid-hulled boats may not come equipped with such flotation chambers, and in such cases it is a good idea for the archaeologist to make provisions for alternatives; Butler (1982) offers many useful suggestions along such lines. Rigid boats usually last longer and are more easily powered than inflatables, but are much more difficult to transport and costly to ship from one place to another unless they are small "car-top" models. Because trailering a boat to an archaeological field location hundreds or thousands of miles from the home institution is a painful and risky business, especially if border crossings must be made, quite often the project boat must be acquired locally.

Most archaeological projects involving small boats are ventures of only a few weeks or months, and in such contexts rental makes much more sense than buying a craft outright. Long-term projects, or those that will be held for a series of successive seasons, may neccessitate that a boat be purchased. The best option in either circumstance is to co-opt a backer's large yacht or houseboat, complete with living facilities and an attendant fleet of small boats to use for project requirements. This may seem an unrealistic or even a facetious suggestion until it is noted that underwater archaeologists have been doing exactly this since the adoption of the aqualung in the 1940s. Most project budgets, of course, would not permit the purchase or even the rental of such equipment, but it is frequently possible to link up with a yachtsman and gain his support, collaboration, and participation. A yachtsman may be interested in adding some excitement and purpose to his cruising experience (as well as obtaining a tax deduction for supporting archaeological research). The archaeologist, on the other hand, is primarily interested in the boat's living accommodations and in its service dinghy which will be used in the visits to the shore and in shoreline explorations. A project backer with his own boat is really the best solution to the problem of access to the boat, for at one stroke both the necessary equipment has been provided, as well as a skilled person who knows how to operate it.

Failing this, the archaeologist must locate his own boat. The first step is to learn as much as possible about the boats being used in the area of study. Boatmen in every region have pretty well worked out over the years the kind of small boat that functions best in the wind, water, tidal or current conditions found in their areas, and this has usually been achieved through constant trial and error, experimentation and correction. Often the safest, cheapest, and easiest solution is to use what the local people use, and either rent, buy or have a local craft built. Nicholas Flemming, for example, did underwater archaeology in Greece using as his dive boat a local fisherman's skiff, Arctic archaeologists routinely use Eskimo kayaks and umiaks, and both of us have done survey work in Latin America using dugout canoes. Dugouts (Figs. 1 and 2) are often commodious, draw very little water and can get into locations where even a standard rowboat cannot easily go.

The decision between importing a boat or securing one at the project location is often made for the archaeologist by others, often because customs registration paperwork is too onerous or import duties are restrictive. Since in most areas few small boats are technically "up for sale" at any given time, the archaeologist may have a difficult time even locating a boat that suits his needs at the project location. Usually boats are not constructed on speculation, but are made only after an order has been tendered. If the project is located in a country with a boat-building tradition, it may be a good idea for the archaeologist to select a complete set of plans at home and deliver them to the boat-builder of his choice at the final destination. Most public libraries have reference works on boat-building and many good plans exist for boats suitable for archaeological purposes (see: Rouse and Rouse 1965; Schock 1952). New plans and new information on the subject constantly appear in many boat-oriented periodicals such as *Yachting, The Rudder, Motor Boating and Sailing, Sea, Cruising World*, and *Small Boat Journal*.

In many areas in most countries, any boat larger than rowboat size (usually about 16 feet in length) must be licensed, registered, and must carry specific kinds of safety equipment. Boatmen in the United States who do not comply with such regulations may be heavily fined or have their craft impounded. Since the rules tend to vary, a legal boat in one jurisdiction may not be legal in another, so the archaeologist must ascertain how this might influence boat selection at the project location. As a rule of thumb, the kinds of safety equipment required for large boats should also be carried in any work boat, no matter how small, for it is a false economy to go out on the water without such equipment just because it may not be required by law.

Few wooden boats in the 8 to 16-foot size range will take much more than a week to construct, and much less time is needed if the seams are only roughly joined and then made water-tight by fiberglassing. Materials may be a problem, however, for in many countries marine or even exterior plywood is impossible to find, as are bronze nails and most other fittings. The archaeologist thus may

Figure 4: Common hull forms. Left to right are shown flat-bottomed, vee-hulled, "cathedral-hulled", round-bottomed, and outrigged hulls.

have to be content with a local craftsman building or renovating some kind of boat that was not his optimum choice. In some cases, such as with dugout canoes, it becomes necessary to order the construction of the boat several months or even a season in advance and to initiate work with a down payment.

Anyone, even an archaeologist, can knock together a plywood river or lake boat in a matter of a few days provided the materials are available and the user is not bothered by the low speed and lack of maneuverability that will result from the finished product. For shallow-water application, a rectangular floor plan with a 4-foot beam and 11-foot overall length (8 feet flat and 3 feet up-angled), 18 to 24-inch high sides outflared at approximately 20° will constitute a work boat that can be powered by an outboard in the 6 to 15 horsepower range. The floor should be of ½ inch marine or exterior plywood (or of ¼ inch plywood if liberally reinforced with longitudinal struts), while the sides can be of ¼ inch with reinforcing chines, gunwales and seats. Seams should be sealed with fiberglass cloth and resin, and the transoms should be of 1-inch plywood or of planking; a mild keel and rear skeg will add stability and some protection for the propeller.

The main criteria for selecting small boats for archaeological purposes are (1) how the boat will be used (i.e., in what kind of water, lacustrine, riverine, etc.); (2) what functions it will be called upon to perform (how large a payload or how many passengers it will be required to carry); (3) how it will be powered (pole, paddle, oar, sail or motor); and (4) how portable it must be out of the water. Economic considerations are of course built into any choice; motor-powered boats, for example, will be the least economical to run in terms of operating expense, but will be most economical of time while sailers will be the opposite.

If the archaeologist is working close to home in an area he can drive to, it may be possible to obtain a trailerable or even a car-top sailer or power boat, but even here it is advisable to use the kind of boat that the locals use so that you do not end up with an inconvenient or even an unsafe boat. Some obvious examples of inappropriate boats can be mentioned. A hull shape (Fig. 4) that is efficient in quiet or shallow water (such as a flat bottom which is ideal for inland rivers) may be very unsafe in the ocean, for it will plow into oncoming waves instead of riding over or through them and may in fact fill with water and swamp after a few minutes. Similarly, a boat with ideal characteristics for deepwater sailing, such as a vee-hulled boat with centerboard or keel and most of its weight on the bottom, 3 to 6 feet under the waterline, is hampered and often useless in places where there are extensive areas of shallow water. Off Belize, for example, centerboard boats are the rule, but even these can touch bottom in some places a mile or two from shore. If the local boatmen have found out long ago what the best and most efficient boat is for their own characteristic water conditions, then the archaeological newcomer should cash in on that knowledge rather than conduct his own trial and error experiments by importing a boat designed for some other set of conditions.

Motive Power

To make the boat go, one has three options: muscle power (oars, paddles, or poles), motor power (either inboard or outboard), and wind power harnessed through sails. Each has certain advantages and disadvantages, and these will also change from region to region and from boat to boat. Many small boats have sails, an outboard or inboard motor, and oars or paddles, and therefore are equipped to cope with differing conditions as the need arises. In this regard, the greater the flexibility of the boat, the more useful it will be for archaeological purposes, and a combination of motive power capabilities is always a good idea. Any outboard-powered boat without oars or at least a paddle, for example, can only be classified as unsafe.

Unless the archaeologist is a true outdoorsman in great physical shape, he will not want to row or paddle a boat, kayak, or canoe for many miles. The work is tiring, forward movement (except with a current) is slow, and worst of all, it demands almost all of your attention, which precludes you from examining the coastline through binoculars or taking notes on your observations. All boat operators, no matter what the principal power source of their craft, should nevertheless have some facility with oars or paddles in order to be able to react correctly in an emergency; some strokes are exhausting and wasteful of energy, while others can be maintained for hours and will get the boat back to shore if the engine quits or the mast breaks.

Wind power is of course the most economical choice in terms of both energy and cost but also requires a greater study investment by the archaeologist. There is a certain amount of skill involved in even sailing a small dinghy (see Fig. 6) back and forth across a sheltered bay, and the archaeologist should have some practice doing basic sailing before he or she attempts to navigate in a field situation. Fortunately, such skill is easy to acquire, and most coastal cities have public classes available at little or no cost. The advantages of using sail are in many cases logistical rather than strictly economical: wind power allows travel through very shallow water in which a propeller shaft might become fouled, and since fuel is not required, problems of supply are greatly lessened and independence increased. Mechanical repairs are kept to a minimum and are easily made by the operator, and the distractions of noise and vibration that usually accompany motor power are absent. Disadvantages of sailboats are, of course, that the wind must be blowing in order to make forward progress, more skill in handling them is required than with other boats, there is a greater risk of capsizing, and close-in maneuverability in contexts such as docking is not always very impressive. Also, in some archaeological situations, sailboats simply cannot be used at all. Most riverine travel, for example, involves so many course changes over short yet narrow distances that wind power cannot be manipulated. Lack of adequate wind or wind from the right heading, of course, can be compensated for by using an auxiliary outboard or by rowing for a while when sails cannot be used.

Outboard motors are in most cases the preferred driving force, and their advantage over muscle or wind in terms of efficiency are remarkable. Equally remarkable are the problems that one can run into purchasing, renting, maintaining and using them. If one is going to be running a certain kind of outboard for any length of time, it is a very good idea to get an owner's manual and shop manual and learn its mechanical characteristics and how to maintain and repair it in the field. Inboards are often much more economical to run than outboards (especially if they are small diesels), but obviously are permanently installed and usually are found only in large and less portable boats. Where outboard motors are unavailable but automobiles are, the best choice may be to convert a car engine to an inboard motor. This is a relatively simple process involving the conversion of the engine to run via hand controls that can be set for constant speeds. The original transmission may be retained, for then the power train will have forward, reverse, and neutral capabilities. A flexible U-joint to connect the propeller and drive shafts can be made simply by cutting short lengths of garden or radiator hose and then clamping their ends to the shaft stubs; direct cooling can be arranged by dispensing entirely with the radiator and installing a screened underwater intake for the water pump. The major problem involved is to ascertain the proper angle for the propeller shaft and the pitch of the propeller itself. Many engines are well suited to such use; the small BMC four-cylinder 1275 cc would be an ideal choice, for example, in a 20 to 25-foot boat, for it only weighs about 250 pounds and produces about 70 horsepower.

The flexibility and ease of transport of outboard motors, on the other hand, makes them very popular. For example, you can have three different boats in three different locations, and use a single outboard to power each of them in rotation. Disadvantages are that such motors are expensive to buy new and are almost always in very poor condition if found used. Few people are willing to rent or loan their outboard to a stranger, much less to a foreigner. A breakdown in a remote area can mean waiting months for parts, and the correct kind of oil for two-cycle models is often hard to find. Outboards will not run well (or sometimes even at all) if the oil/gas mixture is incorrect (normally this is 1:50) or if there is scale, dirt, or water in the fuel. Running an outboard with too low an oil mixture for even only an hour will convert it into a very expensive piece of useless junk.

There is an ideal outboard for every different boat size and hull form, and almost all outboards will accept a variety of propellers varying in pitch for different water or load conditions. It is easy to underpower a small boat but much easier to overpower it; overpowering a boat is not only wasteful of fuel but is also dangerous, for stern flips can result from overlarge engines. For vee-hull or flat bottomed river or deep-water boats in the 12 to 20 foot range, outboards of between 9 and 15 horsepower are entirely adequate for everyday work. Especially heavy loads or rough water conditions may require a larger motor (25 to 30 horsepower) on boats at the extreme of the size range. Shallow-water boat outboards should have short shafts; those for use in deep water or where wave action is common should be equipped with a long shaft. A 15 horsepower long shaft outboard will power a 20-foot boat under light load at about 12 knots in smooth water for four or five hours on a single tank of fuel. This motor weighs only about 100 pounds and can easily be transported by hand or by vehicle.

Any outboard motor should be carefully maintained and properly used. It should normally be run at 3/4 power or less, and certainly no higher than 7/8 power. Cranking the outboard up as high as it will go and then leaving it at its highest RPM for a long time is the surest way to guarantee that no RPMs are going to be produced in a very short while. Engine speed should not be adjudged by the markings on the throttle handle but by changes in tone under different load and water conditions.

Different loads and changes in wave height or in current will render any outboard motor fixed in a specific position either more or less efficient; fortunately, most mounting systems provide for variable outboard shaft-to-transom angles. Using the same boat and outboard for several days in varying conditions will teach the operator which angle is best for light vs. heavy loads, or for running seas as opposed to millpond-like smoothness. In addition to the transom clamps, the outboard should have a security chain or strong cord attached to some strong portion of the boat. On many occasions such chains have made the difference between losing a few minutes and losing the whole engine when a snag or deadhead is hit at high speed. Garbrecht (1979) offers suggestions for improving outboard motor performance.

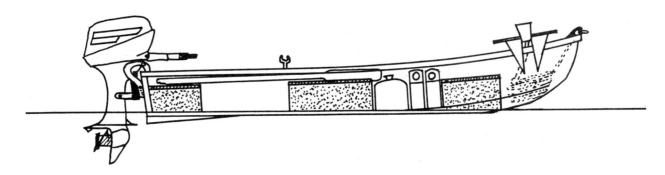

Figure 5: Conventionalized partial cutaway drawing of a 12-foot outboard utility boat. The stippled areas under the seats are flotation chambers, the anchor is wedged over the starboard bow gunwale for quick use in deep water, while the outboard motor is shown with a short shaft more suitable for shallow water. The fuel tank and extra jerrycans are stowed ahead of the central seat, oars are lashed to the inner gunwales at the stern, and all cargo is placed atop the seats or on duckboards over the floor. Such a boat will carry up to 5 persons comfortably.

There are so few moving parts in a two-cycle outboard motor that if it is not running (as is usually the case with second or third-hand motors being offered for sale) it is probably because the unit has been thrashed into junk. Fixing a worn-out motor is usually much more expensive and troublesome than buying a new or used motor in good condition. If wear has increased to the point where compression is down by 1/3 over specifications, a cylinder hone and new rings might fix matters. A compression drop resulting from running with insufficient oil also indicates that the bearings and all other interior parts are shot and that the motor is probably not worth rebuilding. Mechanical damage to the power train, by contrast, is usually easily remedied, for drive shafts, propeller shafts, and propellers can often be fixed or replacements adapted from other engines. Every time a power drop is noted, the spark plugs ought to be pulled and inspected and, if necessary, replaced. A store of spark plug washers should be on hand, for these tend to flatten out after two or three tightenings and lose their ability to seal off escaping cylinder pressure. Each time the outboard motor is taken off the boat, it should be given a quick visual inspection and cleaned and dried, inside and out. It should be stored in an upright position, and if not to be run for some time, it should be run dry of all fuel while in the water or in a drum of oily water. All salt water should be flushed out of it, and salt crusts removed from all electrical wiring and exposed metal surfaces. Especially in salt water, an occasional spray with an aerosol lubricant such as WD-40 is very good insurance against corrosion.

Nothing testifies to the mature status of a river camp more than the pile of wrecked outboard motors that can usually be found in it. A look at the most common mechanical problems will tell the neophyte operator much about the most frequent hazards of the area and the strong and weak points of specific outboards. Nicked, broken or bent propellers bespeak collisions with a rocky or gravelly bottom, or hitting a shoaling shore at excessive speed. Small nicks in the leading edges of prop blades can be filed out, but really hard blows create greater problems. Such prop collisions will throw the drive shaft out of true, or even lock up the crankshaft and blow the cylinder heads off the motor.

As deleterious to any outboard as dragging its propeller over a shallow bottom is running an improper gas/oil mixture. At best (rich) this will lead to sluggishness and to excessive carbon buildup and clogged carburetors. At worst (i.e., lean) this will lead to overheating (and sometimes even fire), then to bearings wearing out or pistons seizing in the cylinders. Very good quality outboard motor oil is expensive but is certainly worth the investment. In out-of-the-way places, unfortunately, it usually cannot be found and something else must be substituted. Any two-cycle oil such as that used for motorcycles will usually do, and even very low viscocity engine oil (such as 10 weight) will serve, but the normal 50:1 mixture ratio will have to be altered. It is a very good idea for one person and one person only to be responsible for mixing the oil and gas. This will ensure that confusion over what was mixed, when, and in what proportions (especially with many different containers in various stages of being emptied) is kept to a minimum.

On the last day of a water-based project directed by one of us, the entire field camp had to be loaded into a flat-bottom boat and powered down the river in time to meet a cargo plane that was coming specifically to pick up our artifact collections. In order to be absolutely certain to make the flight, a second, backup outboard motor had been borrowed in addition to the project's own engine. An inexperienced student, unfortunately, had been detailed to mix the fuel for the last day and produced a combination of one part oil to two parts gas. Needless to say, neither engine would start and the heavily laden boat had to be paddled with shovels 20 miles down to the airstrip.

Another common problem is overheating, from a too-lean gas/oil mixture as already noted, or from plugs gapped too wide, or, most frequently, from a blocked or excessively worn water circulation or cooling system. All modern outboards have a water-pump check system that funnels a thin stream of water through the rear of the casing; the boat operator has only to reach behind the engine periodically to check the pressure of the water stream and its temperature to determine how well the cooling system is working. If this stream becomes excessively hot but its pressure stays the same, some internal problem is developing. If the stream diminishes in volume, the water intake is either clogged or the impeller in the pump itself is worn out. Killing the motor and cleaning out the intake screen will usually solve circulation problems in new engines; rebuilding the water pump is usually necessary in older ones (Hendrickson and Bofill 1982). If outboards are run through water with much suspended silt, sand or sediment in areas such as breakers off sandy beaches, water pumps will wear out rapidly. If the motor has been run through fine silt or sand for only a moment or two, it should be disassembled and its cooling system should be flushed clear of abrasive matter; otherwise, a rebuild may become necessary. Another problem peculiar to the tropics is the propensity for mud-dauber wasps to build nests in various engine apertures; these sometimes seal off the intake and outlets of the cooling system and make disassembly and cleaning necessary. Running with poor quality gas can also clog the gas pump or filter, and it is a good idea to strain all gasoline before it goes into the boat's fuel tank.

The world's best outboards, in terms of dependability, power, economy and parts availability, are the American-made Johnson and Evinrude singles and twins of up to 35 horsepower, and the English-made British Seagull, in various horsepower ratings up to 8 or 9. The Seagull engine is so light that it can be backpacked, so economical that it will run for hours on a gallon of fuel, and so simply made that it can be rebuilt with only three or four basic tools. The Seagull engine is the ideal choice for very small boats such as kayaks or canoes with side mounts, while the larger American motors are excellent for deepwater or river work boats and will stand up to hard daily usage with very little adverse result.

Maintenance and basic repair jobs are greatly simplified by keeping a boat kit handy at all times one is underway. The boat kit should be in a sealed, watertight floating container; a large square biscuit tin or a two gallon plastic mustard or mayonnaise jar with screw top are ideal for this purpose. The container will not only keep basic tools and spare parts dry but also becomes useful when you must swim ashore and need a place to put your wallet, passport, or mail. The boat kit should include the following items:

TOOLS

Spark-plug wrench
Pliers (or vise-grips)
Screwdriver(s)
Knife
Small file
Plug gapper
Sandpaper
Dry towels/rags

SPARES

Propeller
Prop pins (3 or 4)
Starting cord
Spark plugs (2 complete sets)
Plug washers (a dozen or so)
Spray lubricant
Quick-start spray
Wire
Electrician's tape

Safety Equipment

Although certain kinds of equipment (such as paddles) are essential for safe boating, perhaps more important is the attitude of the skipper and his ability to foresee and react to dangerous situations. Some emergencies can occur in the space of an instant, such as unexpected appearances of shoals, reefs, or sandbars, while others such as running out of gas, getting caught out after dark or overloading are the result of cumulative error or of poor planning.

The most basic piece of safety equipment is the life preserver, sometimes called a "personal flotation device." Every boat should have as many life preservers as passengers it carries, and should also contain a few extra for emergency use. A life saving device is useless if it remains in the boat while the person who should have been wearing it falls overboard;   most drownings occur because life preservers were stowed instead of worn. If the crew or passengers are to be the same for the entire project, the archaeological skipper should permanently assign each person a preserver. Thus, if an emergency occurs, no time is lost hunting for a flotation device that someone else says "ought to be there," and each individual has only himself to blame if his own is waterlogged, is missing straps or buckles, or has been left ashore.

In rough water or when danger is anticipated, common sense dictates that the skipper and all passengers wear their life preservers, yet there often seems little reason to do so on a sunny day with no trouble in sight. A compromise that precludes the discomfort and lack of movement resulting from wearing the preserver is to tie a lanyard from the device to each person's ankle or belt, so that if they fall overboard they can quickly recover it and put it on.

There are many different kinds of life preserver available on the market, but some are so inefficient that they are dangerous; Consumer Reports (1982: 410-411) rated the vast majority of those tested as unsafe because of their tendency to turn the swimmer's face down into the water instead of keeping it above the surface. Commercially made life preservers may not be available in out-of-the-way places, yet safety devices are no less neces-

Figure 6: Conventionalized partial cutaway drawing of an eight-foot sailing dinghy. The rudder, centerboard and mast are all removable, which allows for conversion to oar or outboard power. The partial decking at the bow creates a small, protected storage area.

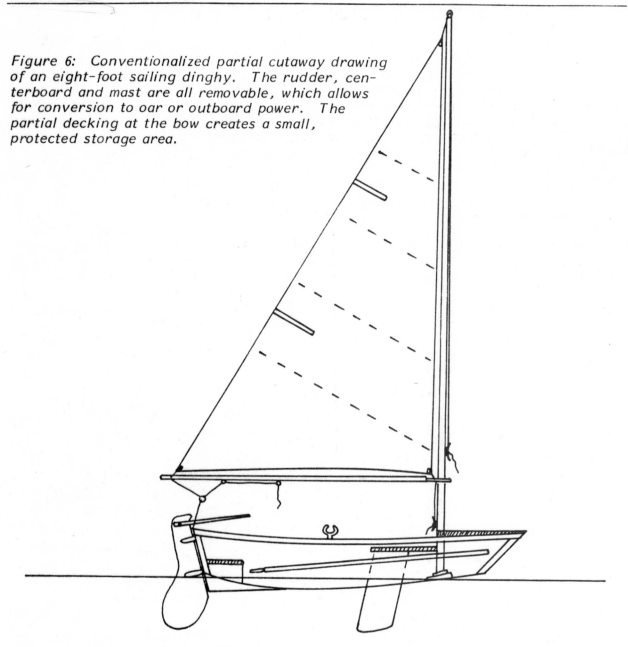

sary. Where custom-fitted vests cannot be obtained, the small boat operator should make his own life preservers, either from inner tubes with attached cords, or by stringing plastic bleach bottles with sealed caps together with nylon rope through their handles. Such home-made equipment should of course be tested under safe conditions before it is relied upon in the field.

Most landsmen overlook another important safety item: swimming fins. A person with a pair of fins can keep afloat even *sans* life preserver for many hours without overexerting himself, and if a long swim to shore is necessary after capsizing, fins may make the difference between safe arrival and drowning. Swimming fins should be lashed together (or at least strapped with a heavy rubber band cut from an inner tube) so that they don't become separated, should float, and should be visible in the dark. They should also be attached to their owner by a lanyard for quick access. Boats that by necessity are anchored some distance offshore because of tidal fluctuations or the possibility of theft are easily reached with fins, and if a boat must be pushed by a swimmer, the job is almost impossible in deep water without fins.

The bailer is another piece of equipment that is often not thought of until it is too late. Bailers should be selected both for the volume of water that can be displaced and for permanence; even a large boat with bilge pumps should have a couple of bailers aboard. A wide plastic basin that can handle a quart or two at a time will probably be the first thing floating away if the boat capsizes; a hole should be drilled through its rim and it should be tied to some stationary object in the boat by means of a long cord. Bailers wtih handles are preferable; these can easily be made from plastic bleach bottles cut diagonally across their bodies. Because such bottles have removable caps, they can also double as funnels for fuel transfers in the boat. Physical comfort is important in selecting bailers for use in extreme conditions (e.g., after a hull puncture or capsizing), because keeping one's cold, wet hand clenched in an unnatural position while bailing for a stretch of three to four hours will eventually lead to exhaustion and result in less water being thrown from the boat.

Signalling devices are now required by law in most U.S. coastal and inland waters for for boats over 16 feet in length. Such devices are either visual or audible, but both rely upon the presence of other boatmen in the neighborhood who can render assistance or upon the local Coast Guard or marine service. Any signalling deivce carried in the boat should be incorporated in the boat kit along with the tools and spares. A number of commercial enterprises offer signalling kits for sale (see, e.g., Olin Products 1980) which satisfy both legal and common sense requirements, but it should be noted that some choices are better than others in specific circumstances. Hand-held flares in small boats are a menance; in outboard-powered boats one can ignite the gas supply (which, by the way, is constantly vaporizing), and it is easy to torch the rigging or sails on a small sailboat. This is not to say that the need for such a device is nonexistent, but a flashlight should be used instead of a flare for signalling after dark. Many people put great stock in aerial flares, usually because they have never had to depend upon them in a life-or-death situation. "Meteor" flares only burn for five or ten seconds and should not be fired unless the person in trouble is certain that someone is around to see them. Parachute flares, of course, are much better and will burn in some cases over a minute, but again, must be seen in order to bring assistance. It should also be noted that flareguns are technically classed as firearms in many countries and the archaeologist trying to import one may find himself in trouble at the port of entry.

Audible signalling devices are usually either compressed-air horns or explosives of one sort or another. To be effective, an audible signal must be heard over the rescue boat's own motor noise, or over the normal sound of wind and surf ashore. For small boats, a few of the compressed-air aerosol can horns can sometimes be useful; alternatives, where permitted, would be large firecrackers or gunshots. The main thing to remember either with a visual or audible signal is that where the signalling device has a limited lifespan (owing to the strength of the batteries or number of cartridges) it must not be used until a rescuer is actually in place and can render assistance.   Apart from mirrors, the best rescue signal of all is a short-wave radio or long-range walkie-talkie. These, unfortunately, cannot be operated without special license in many foreign countries and will also be confiscated at many international borders.

Dangerous Situations and Safety Considerations

All small boats present hazards not encountered on shore. U.S. Coast Guard statistics on boating accidents in this country indicate that the great majority of injuries and fatalities on the water take place in boats under 16 feet in length, identical to those most likely to be used by the field archaeologist. This is no doubt partly because there are so many more small boats in operation than large ones, but it is also due to the fact that small boats are less well adapted to deal with sudden changes in wind, waves, or other weather conditions.

The same Coast Guard estimates note that the primary cause of injury or death is from capsizing or from falling overboard. Collisions and fires are also common and, of course, can often lead to a subsequent capsizing or loss of passengers over the side. Even though the actual percentage of boaters who experience these calamities is quite small in relation to the total number of people on the water, prudence and common sense should be exercised by all persons making use of small boats, especially archaeologists with little or no experience on the water.

The major cause of capsizing and all of its subsequent problems has been shown to be overloading the boat. This means that too many passengers or too much freight was aboard for the size of the vessel. In the United States, small boats are clearly labeled as to their weight and passenger capacity, and the best way to avoid accidents is to carefully observe these limits. Even if extra trips are required, and an archaeological bigwig in the host country is urging you to load seven members of his staff and three of his family into a boat rated for only five, you should not yield to the temptation to "just try it once."

The other most basic precaution concerns weather. If climatological reports are available, they should be heeded. Failing this, you should interview the local boatmen so as to find out about seasonal wind patterns, shifting back eddies, or extreme tides. In some countries small-craft warnings are often posted or announced when the weather will be severe, while in others the archaeological skipper is forced to rely upon his own judgment . In either case, such days are best spent ashore retyping field notes or washing pot sherds, and the rule of thumb should be "if there is doubt, don't venture out". On the Pacific Coast of Lower Central America, where one of us recently spent two field seasons, local boatmen, even those with many years of experience, sometimes get blown out to sea and are lost. An account (probably apocryphal) has it that one seagoing dugout finally came ashore in the Galapagos Islands. Small boat sailors should avoid taking chances and exhibitionistic behavior, for poor judgment or pushing your luck can often have fatal consequences.

Different hazards are presented by river running than by deep-water operation, and the boatman who is used to one set of conditions may not be much accustomed to dealing with the other. Clemens (1980) provides examples of an excellent set of danger situations and their solutions for deep water boating, including what to do if you lose a man overboard, run aground, drag your anchor, and so forth, and his text should be studied and the practice problems run through by anyone who is new to deep water or offshore problems. Common problem situations encountered in inshore waters or on rivers are discussed much more briefly by Farmer(1977), Richey(1979), and Scharff (1960). Some hazards, of course, are the same no matter what kind of water is being traveled over, and suggestions for coping with them are standard.

The most basic safety rule for any craft, no matter its size or where it is operated, is that there be only one captain per boat, who is to be obeyed by all passengers. In a dangerous situation, having more than one person giving directions will confuse and endanger everyone so it is imperative that all people in the boat understand who is in charge and agree to follow his or her directions. Anyone who is unwilling to follow directions should be put ashore at the earliest opportunity and not be allowed in the boat again. Efforts should be made to eliminate linguistic confusion aboard as well, so that quick action can be taken if a problem arises.

Misunderstanding the directions given by an observer in the bow regarding how
to miss a snag can have disastrous results, so before you set off make sure that all
passengers understand one set of basic boating terms. This needn't be in the archaeologist's own native language; in fact, aboard a bilingual or multilingual boat, it
is to the archaeologist's advantage to give orders in the local language in dangerous
situations rather than to hope that his crew understands his own well enough
to react adequately. Hand signals for "slow," "stop," "out-anchor," and the like,
are also quite useful in multilingual situations, as well as under adverse conditions.

The boat operator should take particular pains to find out who among his passengers can swim and who cannot, and to place them in the boat accordingly. He
should also make certain that all nonswimmers have their life preservers on and their
shoes off or at least unlaced. In addition, the operator should impress upon his crew
that nobody is simply a "passenger" in a small boat, because all must occasionally be
called upon to help by bailing, by shifting their weight to make running more efficient
or safer, to haul in or put out the anchor, or to help work the boat out past the
surfline or in close enough for loading. Unfortunately, most of these activities involve getting wet to some degree, and the natural tendency of those accustomed to
traveling in comfort is to keep from getting wet at all. The operator must be able to
count upon all passengers to react very quickly to any problem, such as the possibility of being swamped or running aground; any passenger who will not participate
because he or she does not want to get wet should not be in the boat. Passengers,
especially those in the bow should be constantly on the lookout for flotsam, deadheads,
snags, shallows, or sandbars that the operator at the stern cannot see. Each
passenger should be taught how to get the anchor over the side and to kill the engine
or drop the sails with only a few seconds' warning, and how to bring the prop up
in shallow water by shifting weight forward.

The archaeologist should also be familiar with his boat's behavior when swamped
and should intentionally swamp it in calm, shallow water (without the outboard attached,
of course) if it is a small craft. Knowing its handling characteristics is crucial.
Does it sink like a brick? Does it float with any freeboard (and therefore can be bailed
out), or does it float sluggishly just below the surface of the water? Can it be nav-
igated (and therefore paddled or pushed back to shore), or is it completely immobile
(and thus must eventually be abandoned)? The buoyancy of almost all boats can be
increased by constructing permanent flotation chambers (see Fig. 5). All passengers should be instructed to stay with the boat even if it swamps or capsizes.

Capsizing or other dangerous situations often occur because passengers un-
advisedly attempt to enter or leave the boat at the wrong time. Too many people
trying at once to come aboard or to jump ashore without getting wet can create
real problems. Many ribs have been cracked and legs broken by people who misjudged their entrance into a pitching boat, and the operator should be heeded and
obeyed. Passengers should not be allowed to disembark before the boat comes to a
full stop. People commonly try to jump out so as to lighten the load, help guide
the boat in, or because they are in a hurry; misjudgments here can swamp the
boat, or result in the person in the water being run over and chopped up with the
propeller. Some maladroits will only put one leg into the water from a moving boat,
and are often surprised to find that they are flipped out from the drag. Such people often are wearing expensive cameras, or manage to snag the other foot in the
project field notes, radio, etc. and take such equipment with them over the side.

The small boat operator should practice man-overboard drills with each of the
project members. This familiarizes everyone with the mechanics of working the

boat around so as to pick someone out of the water. Most landsmen do not realize how difficult this maneuver is, especially when there is a heavy sea or a current is running strongly. Immediately after contact is made, all forward power should be stopped, either by dropping the sail or killing the motor. Trying to haul a waterlogged individual aboard a small boat over the stern transom (usually the lowest in any boat) with the engine down is very dangerous; people should only come over the side gunwales.

Chart-reading is almost impossible in a small boat that is pitching and tossing, or taking on water, or exposed to the wind; it is, however, relatively easy in the comfort of the field camp ashore. The boat operator should study all available maps and charts of the river course, lakeshore outline, or seacoast before he gets near the water, and should be able to trace his route, local hazards, and important features from memory. He should also test himself by drawing maps from memory on pieces of paper and comparing them to the originals. If he does this, he will know exactly where he is when trouble arises nine times out of ten and will make the correct decision about how to get safely ashore. For maintaining a constant heading if and when this is necessary , the operator can consult either a hand-held compass (tied around his neck, of course, with a lanyard) or a semipermanent one affixed to the boat. A relatively inexpensive backpacker's compass (such as the Silva type 7NL, which only costs $8) can be screwed or clamped to a seat, a brace, or some other fixture, or even to a removable post. This kind of compass has a rotating dial that will allow one to set a course and then steer the boat along the desired compass heading; even a nonliterate crewman can steer correctly by simply lining up the arrows.

One of the most basic safety precautions that should be taken regardless of the kind of location or type of boat is to make certain that you have someone ashore who is aware of your intended destination and the estimated time of arrival. In this way, if you fail to arrive at the designated time, steps can be taken to begin a search for you or to help you in. If the people ashore know you are overdue, they will be watching for a flare, listening for a shot, or will respond to a signal. If it is dark, they should build a signal fire to guide you in, wave flashlights, or wade out and hold a coleman latern up for you to aim towards. Under no circumstances should anyone plan to go out into rough water in a small boat after dark, unless it is an emergency and you are searching for someone else. The shore people should know enough about how to operate a boat that they can put themselves in your place if there seems to be trouble and respond accordingly.

As important as knowing where you are at all times while afloat, is knowing how long it takes to get from place to place. One of us was running a project of over a year's duration some time ago on a river in the Central American rain forest; the field camp had to be supplied by boat from the nearest roadhead and airstrip 32 kilometers downriver. Part of each crewmember's normal responsibility was to run the boat down every few days to pick up supplies, mail, and news, and to drop off and pick up new personnel. With the boat lightly loaded and only the operator in it, the roadhead could sometimes be reached after only 90 minutes of running with the current. Fighting the current upstream with a full load of supplies, additional crew members back from the big city, and several extra tanks of gas sometimes turned the return trip into a 5 to 6 hour marathon afloat. Timing was therefore important, and the various jobs that had to be done at the roadhead (such as buying supplies, getting gasoline, etc.) had to be completed by noon. Otherwise, the boat would not have enough time to make it back to camp before dark, for it was pitch black by about 6 or 6:30 pm. On two separate occasions a person running the boat misjudged the time available and tarried too long at the roadhead by having lunch; he paid the penalty by spending two very cold, wet nights in the boat tied up on the sandbar nearest to him when night fell.

A different student, in the same boat on his first solo voyage, went downriver in a dense fog and unknowingly bypassed the roadhead because he couldn't see the riverbanks. Because this person knew how long it should have taken him to reach his destination, he decided that he had gone too far and decided to turn back. He had, in fact, drifted over the border into the neighboring country and was fortunate to escape incarceration and confiscation of the boat. Both of these situations were somewhat comical in their riverine contexts, for misjudging time or distance or the contents of your fuel tank need not be too serious when you can always tie up to the bank. If the same situations had occurred on a deep-water project, however, either student may have lost his life.

River travel can be very dangerous, and while not as many river accidents end in drownings as do offshore ones, a lack of vigilance will result in disaster much more quickly than on an open bay. If the project boat is going to be running along the same stretch of river over an extended period, it is a good idea to establish safety stations every 10 kilometers or so, or at least halfway. These would contain hidden fuel caches in case you run out, and some kind of shelter. Unfortunately, you cannot just tie up to the bank in a deep-water situation and walk home as you can if working on an inland waterway, but by the same token you cannot rig a sea-anchor and fix your dead motor or replace your torn sail on a swift-running river as you can on open water, for you will soon ram a snag or capsize. At one point, one of us was drifting downstream in a small boat and became tangled broadside to the current against a wall of tropical vines; it was only the rapid weight transfer of passengers that averted swamping.

While much attention is usually given to passenger safety while afloat, surprisingly little is devoted to protecting the boat while it is not in use. A lightweight, portable boat is best protected by hauling it out of the water and airing it upside-down where it can be kept free of wet rot and weeds; an added benefit of this is that the owner need not be concerned that his craft will sink at its moorings or that another boat will collide with it. Boats in daily use on the water, on the other hand, are usually left afloat and are tied up to some stationary object ashore or are anchored in place. Few experiences are worse than getting up in the morning and looking out to sea only to find that your boat, which you anchored the night before, is nowhere in sight; such a situation, fortunately, usually only occurs from negligence, not fate.

Beyond the obvious suggestions that could be made (such as how one should not drop anchor in a busy shipping lane, or just off an exposed, rocky coastline during hurricane weather) are some rather more subtle points for consideration. The operator has no less important a responsibility to the boat than to his passengers, and he or she alone must check to see that the boat is secure at the end of each day. This means that the status of the ropes and knots and the condition of the cleats, stanchions and posts is positively known at all times. Figure 7 provides a basic review of the more useful boating knots; temporary knots, such as the clove hitch, should always be replaced by permanent knots if the boat is to be left for any period of time.

The most common mistake made while anchoring any boat, or in tying up to a mooring post ashore, is failing to leave adequate slack in the line. This practice is not much of a problem for weekend sailors who moor at floating docks; every change in water level experienced by the boat is also paralleled by the dock, and thus the length of the line is immaterial. Tying up to a fixed object on shore, however, is a different matter. The constant tugging and pulling exerted by most boats on their mooring ropes can easily slip poorly tied knots, break off small branches, or even uproot saplings, so careful selection of the knot and the mooring post is advisable. Even where there is no usual tidal shift, lots of slack in the line is a good idea. One of us had the experience of tying up to a firmly anchored post on the bank next to a very large tropical river and leaving only about 8 feet of slack in the painter. That night, torrential rains in the mountains many miles to the south created widespread flooding, which of course was eventually channeled into the river in question. Even though the boat was perhaps 40 kilometers downstream from the rainstorm, the water level was raised 12 feet overnight, and the boat eventually stood on its nose because of the short painter, then filled with water and sank. It took seven people hauling to raise it high enough so that bailing could begin. Where an anchor is used near shore in a deep-water situation, it is a good idea to have at least a 10 to 15-foot length of chain as an anchor lead before the anchor rope begins. This adds important weight, and keeps the anchor on a rough bottom.

A very wide margin of safety is necessary while anchoring offshore in an area with substantial tides. During another episode in a different archaeological field project, the operator delegated the job of anchoring to a volunteer instead of doing it himself, and the neophyte paid out too little line. There was a tidal drop of 10 feet where the boat was anchored and around 15 feet of line was paid out. This would have been barely adequate in calm water. What the neophyte did not plan for was a series of 5-foot waves and the pitching of the 20-foot-long boat during the night, which simply picked the anchor off the bottom and walked the boat off with it. This caused a collision with another boat anchored nearby, and brought both of them up on the beach stuck fast in the sand. The rule of thumb is to pay out as much line as you have and to know your knots. The time to learn how to tie a bowline or a fisherman's bend is during a period of relaxation ashore, not in a pitching boat in the rain at night.

Although the danger of losing a boat is greatest from the vicissitudes of mother nature, thievery must also be anticipated and guarded against. Only the naive and trusting fail to take their gas line or rudder with them when they leave their boat unattended. If the craft is to be left for a long period of time, anything stealable should be carried ashore and locked up. Most boatmen fortunately have a very highly developed sense of honor; this is especially true in isolated areas, where each looks after the other's boat and posessions. In regions where boats are scarce every operator quickly comes to recognize each craft on the water and becomes acquainted with its operator. Near international borders, however, it is always easy to blame some foreigner from up the coast or down the river when something turns up missing, and the incidence of theft in such areas is very high. In one frontier situation, the outboard motor, gas, oars, and all other removable equipment had to be hauled every day by hand more than a kilometer from its storage depot to the boat (Dillon, this volume, figure 1). The boat itself had the national flag of the country of origin painted on its bow decking so that if spotted from the air out of national waters it would be recognized as stolen.

Most deep-water boats of rigid construction have drain plugs that allow bilge water to be pulled out of the hull during fast running; the best systems have an exterior and an interior plug, and both plugs have lanyards attached to them so that they don't get lost. The operator removes the outer plug before starting out, and then the inner one after he has reached the speed at which the water is sucked out. Removing all of the bilgewater from a small boat either through bailing or through use of the drain plug can make a major improvement in performance. Two inches of water in the bottom of the boat can weigh as much as several passengers or a full load of cargo, and can decrease fuel economy by 20 to 30% and add up to 15 or 20 minutes to a trip that normally takes an hour. If one has been running a boat for

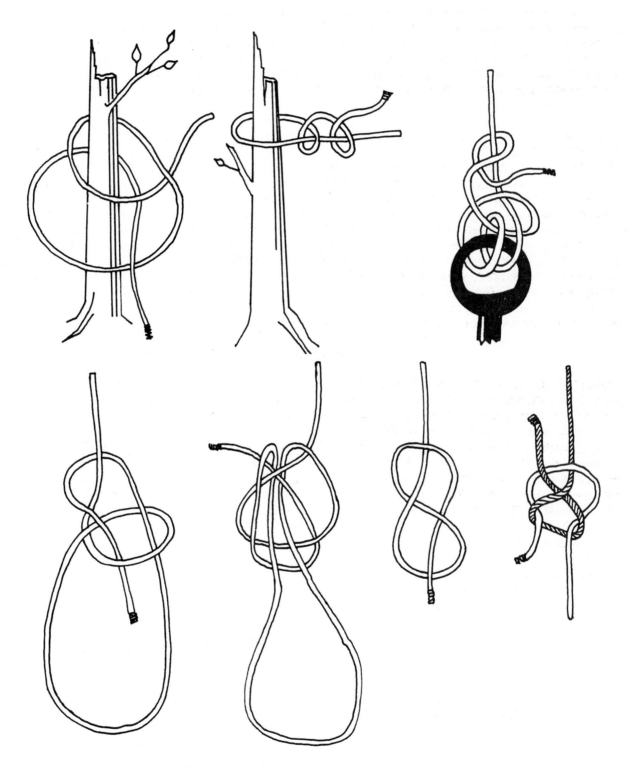

Figure 7: Essential small boat knots. A: Clove hitch; B: Two half hitches (both for tying up to a stationary mooring post); B: Fisherman's bend (for securing the anchor line); C: Bowline; D: Butterfly (both for creating a noose that will not slip); E: Figure eight knot (for putting a "stopper" in a length of line); F: Sheet bend (for joining two lines together).

several hours, it is easy to forget that the drain plug is out; the operator should always check to see that both openings are closed before leaving the boat. On one occasion, one of us let an associate take the project boat out on what was to be that person's first solo voyage. After congratulating the associate for his successful trip the boat was revisited and was found to be lacking both drain plugs; about an inch of freeboard was remaining, and the outboard motor was about to be given a salt-water bath.

The loading of archaeological cargo should be supervised by the archaeologist himself, and the smaller the size of the boat, the more important this task becomes. Nonliterate workmen and nonthinking volunteers can usually be counted upon to put the project field notes in the bottom of the boat, and then to pile heavy gunnysacks full of potsherds atop them; the result is usually a sodden mass of running ink and paper cemented solid. Any materials that should be kept dry must be placed on the seats where they will not be soaked by the bilgewater; these should be guarded a-gainst spray by wrapping with plastic bags. Before entering the boat for any trip, the archaeologist should think how his excavated materials, notes, camera, etc. might be saved if the boat swamps or he gets caught out in a squall. Putting expensive equipment such as transits, or delicate materials such as exposed film in floating boxes or in water-tight containers inside life preservers is a good idea, and in rainy areas enough tarpaulins should be available inside the boat to cover the entire load.

Conclusion

While the difficulties in doing archaeology with small boats as basic transportation may have seemed overwhelming at times in the preceding discussion, and the cautions sometimes overabundant, it should be reiterated that all necessary skills can be mastered in only a few days or weeks. The investment of time should pay off handsomely and enable the inquisitive archaeologist to explore hitherto unreachable areas or to mount field projects that would have been deemed impossible before. A more general acceptance of small boats as an important logistical aid to field archaeology cannot help but result in an overall increase in the amount of archaeological knowledge about ancient peoples in both inland and coastal environments.

REFERENCES CITED

Beals, Ralph L.
  1982 Fifty Years in Anthropology.
        Annual Review of Anthropology, 1982, 11: 1-23.

Brothwell, Don R.
  1965 Digging Up Bones: The Excavation, Treatment and Study of Human
        Skeletal Remains.
        British Museum, Staples Printers, Ltd., St. Albans, Herts.

Butler, Paul
  1982 Keeping Her Afloat: Positive Flotation for Your Boat.
        Small Boat Journal, no. 26, September, 1982; 36-38.

Caffey, J.
  1967 Pediatric X-ray Diagnosis. Fifth Edition.
        The Year Book Publishers, Inc., Chicago.

Chilton Book Company
  1971 Chilton's Auto Repair Manual: 1954-1963.
        Automotive Book Department, Chilton Book Company, Radnor, Pennsyl-
        vania.

  1980 Chilton's Repair and Tune-Up Guide: Ford Pick-ups, 1965-80.
        Chilton Book Company, Radnor, Pennsylvania.

Clemens, John
  1980 Contingency Seamanship: Coping with the Unexpected in Harbor and
        at Sea.
        Ziff-Davis Books, New York, N.Y.

Clymer Publications
  1980 Chevy & GMC Pickups, 1967-1980: Shop Manual.
        Clymer Publications, Arleta, California.

Consumer Reports
  1982 Consumer Reports Tests Life Jackets.
        Consumer's Union, August, 1982, Mount Vernon, New York; 410-412.

Crosby, Harry
  1974 The King's Highway in Baja California.
        Copley Press, Inc., Salt Lake City, Utah.

  1975 Red-On-Granite Rock Painting in the Sierra de San Borja,
        Baja California.
        Pacific Coast Archaeological Society Quarterly, Vol. 11, no. 1.
        Costa Mesa, California

Dillon, Brian D.
n.d.   Report on the Boundary Test Program Carried Out at LAn-218,
       The Corbin Tank Archaeological Site on Mulholland Drive, City
       of Los Angeles, California.
       Unpublished ms., UCLA Archaeological Survey (1981).

Donnan, Christopher
1965   Moche Ceramic Technology.
       Nawpa Pacha, Vol. 3, University of California, Berkeley: 115-138.

Dreizen, S., C.N. Spirakis and R.E. Stone
1964   The Influence of Age and Nutritional Status on "bone scar"
       Formation in the Distal End of the Growing Radius.
       American Journal of Physical Anthropology, Vol. 22:   295-306.

Farmer, Charles J.
1977   The Digest Book of Canoes, Kayaks and Rafts.
       DBI Books, Inc., Northfield, Illinois.

Frink, Maurice with Casey Barthelmess
1965   Photographer on an Army Mule.
       University of Oklahoma Press, Norman.

Garbrecht, Gary
1979   Outboard Power: How to Let it Rip.
       Motor Boating and Sailing, April, 1979; 104-6, 173-5.

Garn, S.M. and P.M. Schwager
1967   Age Dynamics and Persistent Transverse Lines in the Tibia.
       American Journal of Physical Anthropology, Vol. 27:   375-377.

Georgano, G.N.
1968   The Complete Encyclopedia of Motorcars: 1885-1968.
       E.P. Dutton & Co., Inc., New York.

Gray, P.H.
1967   Radiography of Ancient Egyptian Mummies.
       Medical Radiography and Photography, Vol. 43:   34-44.

Harris, H.A.
1931   Lines of Arrested Growth in the Long Bones in Childhood:
       The Correlation of Histological and Radiographic Appearances
       in Clinical and Experimental Conditions.
       The British Journal of Radiology, 55 (47):   561-589 and 4(48): 622-641/

Hendrickson, Ray and Dave Bofill
1982   Inside Outboards: Water Pumps Impell Consideration.
       Small Boat Journal, no. 26, September, 1982; 82-84.

Howard, Robert West
1965   The Horse in America.
       Follett Publishing Company, Chicago.

Hudson, D. Travis
    1981 To Sea or Not to Sea: Further Notes on the "Oceangoing" Dugouts
          of North Coastal California.
          Journal of California and Great Basin Anthropology, vol. 3, no. 2,
          Banning, California; 269-282.

King, Linda
    1969 The Medea Creek Cemetery (LAn-243): An Investigation of Social
          Organization from Mortuary Practices.
          Archaeological Survey Annual Report, Vol. 11, University of
          California, Los Angeles, 23-68.

Kroeber, Alfred L.
    1925 Handbook of the Indians of California.
          Bureau of American Ethnology, Bulletin 78.
          Smithsonian Institution, Washington, D.C.

MacLeod, Murdo J.
    1973 Spanish Central America: A Socioeconomic History, 1520-1720.
          University of California Press, Berkeley.

McHenry, Henry
    1968 Transverse Lines in Long Bones of Prehistoric California Indians.
          American Journal of Physical Anthropology, Vol. 29: 1-17.

Meggers, B.J. and C. Evans
    1957 Archaeological Investigations at the Mouth of the Amazon.
          Smithsonian Institution, Bureau of American Ethnology, Bulletin 167.
          Washington, D.C.

Millon, R., B. Drewitt, and G. Cowgill
    1973 The Teotihuacan Map: 2 Volumes.
          University of Texas Press, Austin, Texas.

Mosley, M., and C. Mackey
    1974 Twenty-four Architectural Plans of Chan Chan, Peru.
          Peabody Museum of American Archaeology and Ethnology,
          Harvard University, Cambridge, Massachusetts.

Office of the Chief Signal Officer
    1911 Drill Regulations for Field Companies of the Signal Corps.
          Washington, Government Printing Office.

Olin Products
    1980 Boating Safety, the Law, and You.
          Olin Safety Products Operation, East Alton, Illinois.

Richey, David
    1979 The Small-Boat Handbook.
          Thomas Y. Crowell, New York.

Robinson, Arthur E. and Randall D. Sale
1969 Elements of Cartography.
J. Wiley and Sons, New York.

Rouse, Donald and David Rouse
1965 You Can Build Your Own Sailboat.
Harper and Row, Publishers, New York.

Saiz, M.
1968 Diccionario de Mecanica: Ingles-Espanol.
Minerva Books, Ltd., New York.

Scharff, Robert
1960 The Complete Book of Outboard Cruising.
G.P. Putnam's Sons, New York.

Schock, Edson J.
1952 How to Build Small Boats.
A.S. Barnes and Company, New York.

Schwager, P.M.
1968 The Frequency of Appearance of Transverse Lines in the Tibia
in Relation to Childhood Illnesses.
Abstracted in American Journal of Physical Anthropology, Vol. 29: 120.

Scientific Resource Surveys (SRS)
n.d. Archaeological Field Test Report on Sites Ora-458, Ora-485, Ora-486,
Ora-488, Ora-507 located in the Upper Aliso Creek Area of Orange
County. Unpublished ms., UCLA Archaeological Survey, (1977).

Sclar, Deanna
1976 Auto Repair for Dummies.
Mc Graw-Hill Book Company, New York

Squier, Ephraim G.
1852 Nicaragua: Its People, Scenery, Monuments, and the Proposed
Interoceanic Canal.
Appleton Publishing Company, New York.

Stephens, John L.
1841 Incidents of Travel in Central America, Chiapas and Yucatan: 2 volumes.
Harper and Brothers, New York .

Tomlinson, Charles and Sarah Tomlinson
1859 Lessons from the Animal World.
Society for Promoting Christian Knowledge, London.

Topfer, F. and W. Pillewizer
1966 The Principles of Selection.
The Cartographic Journal, 3: 10-16.

Van Horn, D. M. and J.P. Brock
    n.d. Investigations at LAn-669 (the Daon Site): Surface Collection and Test
        Excavations at a Prehistoric Chumash Camp.
        Unpublished ms., UCLA Archaeological Survey, (1981).

Van Horn, D.M. and J.R. Murray
    n.d. Excavations at Ora-486 and 507 near El Toro: An Intermediate Plant
        Processing Station and Quarry. Unpublished ms., UCLA Archaeological
        Survey, (1980).

Wachtell, J.K.
    1978 Soil Survey of Orange County and Western Part of Riverside County,
        California.
        United States Department of Agriculture: Soil Conservation Service
        and Forest Service, Washington, D.C.

Waar, Bob
    1975 Off-Road Handbook: With Back Country Travel Tips.
        H.P. Books, Tucson, Arizona.

Wauchope, Robert
    1974 They Found the Buried Cities: Exploration and Excavation in the
        American Tropics.
        University of Chicago Press, Chicago, Illinois.

Wells, G.
    1961 A New Approach to Ancient Disease.
        Discovery, Vol. 22: 526-531.